Lucky Man:
A Life Lived One Shot at a Time

Captain Stephen A. Luckey

© 2021 Stephen A. Luckey
Print: ISBN 978-0-578-90452-8
eBook ISBN 978-0-578-90455-9

First edition.

Cover design: Woody Myers

Printed in the United States of America

Lucky Man:
A Life Lived One Shot at a Time

For Jeannie

Table of Contents

Foreword: Lucky Man

"Courage is being scared to death but
saddling up anyway."
—John Wayne, from *The Cowboys*

Looking back as far as I can remember, my life story has been filled with adventure. It has been a life regularly inscribed with danger and violence demanding quickdraw response and a steady trigger finger. It has also been a life marked by joy and a great deal of laughter, occasional absurdity, and a lot of comradery.

I can't tell you why, but so often fate has taken me into the heat of action—from a childhood marked frequently by searching for those lost *in* the woods and those lost *to* the woods to an adulthood discovering the tactics necessary to confront a newly encountered age of terrorism. I have been shot and I have done the shooting. With disturbing frequency, I have faced circumstances in which the outcome could have gone either way, yet as I close out my eighth decade, I'm still here to tell my story. Mostly, I've been lucky. In the end, that's how I see my life, one of good fortune largely shaped through opportunities provided by others who believed in me.

Guns have been front and center in my life. Two of the common denominators present throughout my life have been a natural ability to shoot well and to take the shot with calmness and resolve when situations demanded it. Guns, and their role in hunting and security and their larger place in the culture I was born in, have brought me mentors and friends, comradery in recreation and comradery in war. They have placed me in positions to land jobs, to get ahead, and to experience regularly situations that most people find only in the books they read and movies they watch. Employing guns as part of my stock in trade has forced me to face fear and given me a tool that I could wield to overcome it.

From the time I was old enough to shoot a gun without having its recoil knock me on my ass, my dad taught me to respect a weapon's power, its usefulness, and its safe use. For reasons I cannot explain, by adolescence, I was a better shot than my father, who was no slouch, having used his ability to put game in the meat locker to feed our family. As a teenager I set a world record for the 200-yard sitting rapid fire in competitions at Camp Perry, Ohio using an M1, and once I joined the Marines after college, I won the Marine Corps rifle championships. The ability to shoot well in tense situations placed a bounty on my head by the Viet Cong during my Vietnam tour in 1966 – 1967 and the experience as a Marine Corps sniper there provided, alongside the special operations and counter-intelligence missions with which I was assigned, experience that eventually led to me being used as a counter-terrorism operative by the FBI. Those experiences, in turn, guided the long arc of my career as a commercial pilot for Northwest Airlines and eventually to the role as Chair of the Airline Pilots Association Security Committee in the years preceding and immediately following the September 11th terrorist attacks on our country. And when my country called on the leadership of a gun-wielding, bare-knuckled fighter, seat-of-the-pants pilot from the backwoods of Pennsylvania to help guide the war on terrorism that was taking place in the sky, I was proud to answer the call.

I don't know if it was because of dumb luck or my lifelong need for speed and adventure, but I manned the lines at forest fires, participated in arrests, waded debris-filled flood waters, broke up fights and initiated others—all by the age of fifteen. Those experiences of my childhood and youth in the midst of trauma prepared me to face later experiences with calmness and confidence. I have survived firefights, assassination attempts, and mid-air collisions. I have looked into the eyes of skyjackers while they held innocent people hostage. I have spent more time than is natural in the presence of death. Many of the indelible memories of my life are etched there because of its proximity. Instead of becoming morbid or a fatalist, while death has fascinated me in what some might see as an unnatural way, it has provided me a zest for living. I suppose I have something in common with undertakers in that regard. I see life as a privilege, and as such, it is something that must be treated with great respect. These beliefs have been cemented by accepting missions where I have often been asked to take action to preserve the lives of others.

Much of the work I have undertaken offers no glory and no accolade. Some of it I'm not permitted to talk about with any detail. Such is the dirty work of protecting lives and maintaining freedom. I've done my best never to shrink from this call, to saddle up and ride into the unknown. Despite living close to trauma at critical turning points of my life, more often I have experienced the laughter of sharing a joke or a hunt or a swig of whiskey with good friends, experienced the love of good women, felt the pride watching my four children grow into successful happy adults, and delighted in the thrill of riding a spirited horse, racing a powerful car, or throttling up a jet. All in all, I'd say I've been a lucky man.

This book tells the stories of many of those adventures and offers my attempt to understand, as best as I am able, why fate put me at the center of them. Because I've counted myself lucky, I've tried to pass along some of what finding myself in the heat of the action has taught me and how it has shaped my life.

A Boy in the Woods

"Earth and sky, woods and fields, lakes and rivers, the mountain and the sea, are excellent schoolmasters, and teach some of us more than we can ever learn from books."—John Lubbock

I had something close to a storybook childhood in the woods of eastern Pennsylvania, growing up among the lakes and summer camps of the Poconos. Or maybe I only saw it as storybook, for along with freedom and adventure, room to roam, and natural beauty, the Lehigh Valley offered up plenty of hard winters, tough living, and tragedy. As a result, communities like Stroudsburg, Saw Creek, Hunters Range, and other towns in the Pennsylvania mountains provided me a unique education that set the rest of my life in motion.

Several of my formative years were spent in and around Promised Land State Park, where my dad, Alvin "Chick" Luckey, was the Pennsylvania Department of Forests and Wildlife ranger for several years. Promised Land covers 3,000 acres and is nearly surrounded by 12,000 acres of the Delaware State Forest, and in the 1940s and '50s it was largely a wild, free place with dense woods and thick bogs frequented by black bears and abundant with deer and other game. During the early years of my family's time at Promised Land we lived in the ranger station where my dad was often the lone authority for miles around. Because of that, or perhaps because of my mom's famous pies (she often baked a dozen a day), the ranger station was the hub of all activity.

Although my mom, Mabel (Bush) Luckey, was famous for her pies, people came for her company as well. Smart and tireless, she was probably the only person capable of keeping her husband in line.

Whether at home managing both the station and my dad, working as accountant for the Pat Ridge Goodyear Tire dealer, helping her Aunt Maggie run an eight-room boarding house up on Shiny Mountain, or volunteering as president of the Pennsylvania Republican Women, my mother knew how to cultivate contacts and charm people. More than once it was my mom who found my dad a job and helped us to move up in life. She was the stalwart figure in a place of frequent calamity, helping to make the ranger station the center of people's lives and a place of community and comfort.

All the news of the area passed through our doors, and in times of emergency the station became a kind of impromptu command center. Lost hikers, lost children, suicide victims, hunting accidents, weather events—every manner of incident was reported through the ranger station, and most of the time it was my father, usually with me in tow, who coordinated the response. My training in reacting to dramatic events started young.

While I essentially "came of age" in Promised Land, we didn't move there until I was in fourth grade. I was born in Emmaus, Pennsylvania. Dad worked for the Mack Truck Company in nearby Allentown and my mom did whatever she had to in order to make ends meet: working as a chamber maid, waitress, laundress, and seamstress, among other demanding occupations.

Dad dealt with low blood pressure and general fatigue caused by working extended hours in difficult factory conditions. He was seriously underweight, tipping the scales at an emaciated 125 pounds when I was born on March 8, 1940. Many of his health concerns were linked to a difficult childhood. Born into a large, poor family, his mother died giving birth to his youngest sister. Overwhelmed, my grandfather placed Dad and his brother in a Lutheran orphanage in Topton, Pennsylvania while other siblings were sent to live with extended family. Life in the orphanage was tough, something he liked to frequently remind me of during my own childhood. The orphanage scarred him and toughened him, and he passed along a few scars and a good deal of toughness to me. Learning to scrape something together out of nothing and then make it a viable concern was something at which my father was an expert. His tenacity and innovativeness were attributes central to how he went about educating me.

Dad was rescued from the factory by his mother-in-law in 1944. My grandmother, Janet Miller-Bush, was a dynamic, adventurous divorcee and a successful businesswoman in a male-dominated world. She was definitely not typical of most of the local women her age—she even had her own square-dance band where she played the fiddle. Her tactics might not have placed her in the society pages of city newspapers, but she used her encounters with men to maintain the relationships that allowed her business to succeed. Close to the New York border and within a couple hours of Philadelphia, her venue at the Saw Creek Club catered to successful businessmen looking to get out of the cities of New York, New Jersey, and Pennsylvania.

My grandmother also ran a hunting and fishing camp at Saw Creek, but because the war was on and men were in short supply—either serving overseas or drawn into manufacturing centers to fuel the war effort—she urgently needed help. Her invitation to my father to leave the factory floor for the fresh air of the Poconos set the rest of his professional life in motion, which it ultimately did for my life as well. I have never known greater happiness than being among those mountains.

My dad, a licensed plumber and electrician, did maintenance and repairs, cut heaps of necessary firewood, and generally kept things running at the Saw Creek Club. Wood cutting was a full-time business since the entire camp was heated by old box stoves. The Club was off the grid, using a Delco generator plant and DC batteries to provide lights. We cut ice in the winter, then stacked it in a stone icehouse packed with sawdust to use for refrigeration in the summer. My mom continued the kinds of duties she'd become accustomed to in Emmaus, only now in the employ of her mother.

I remember the Saw Creek Club as a bustling place, one that seemed to belong to an earlier age—but that was just fine with me. Every day felt like an adventure. Times were hard during those war years what with rationing and a dearth of clients since so many men were shipped overseas. Winters in the eastern Pennsylvania mountains were often severe, but my grandmother did whatever was required to keep the family and the business alive.

My dad was cut from a similar cloth. Usually he relied on tools he innately had in order to get the job done, and while he was quick to learn new skills by the seat of his pants, he also took mail-order courses to expand his knowledge when he had the money and the time. Dad was a trapper from childhood, and while those abilities kept us afloat for a lot of years, sometimes things got pretty lean. We were no strangers to eating rattlesnake when food was scarce and snakes weren't. One awful winter, when I was about three or four years old, food was in such short supply that people around the Lehigh Valley were starving to death. Dad took matters into his own hands. Through an old contact from one of his trap lines, he met a man who owned an old horse. Dad killed that horse, butchered the animal, and shared the meat with several families that might not have eaten otherwise.

Times weren't always that tough though. In better years and in prosperous times after the war, my dad expanded the ways in which he made a living, reinforcing the skills that trapping and hunting had instilled in him while passing those things along to me. I grew up not really differentiating the hard work required by the woods from the joy I found being in them. The forest served as both a grocery store and a playground for as long as I could remember.

After a time, my mom landed Dad his first job with the Pennsylvania Department of Forestry and Wildlife as a state forest ranger. We moved a few miles up Route 402 to Hunters Range in 1945, settling into the same station where her father, Arch Bush, was ranger when she was a child. At Hunters Range we lived close to my great-grandmother's homestead and we were also near my Uncle Miller at the Girard College Camp. Beyond hunting and fishing camps that were so familiar to my upbringing, the Pocono Mountains were home to resorts, golf courses, retreat-style summer camps for underprivileged city kids, and other philanthropic institutions like Girard. While kids from cities had the good fortune to spend parts of their summers in that natural play land, I got to live there all year long.

Grandmother Miller lived with her son Peter. Uncle Pete was a talented blacksmith and a dedicated alcoholic. Their spread was a beautiful, isolated place. A running spring served as refrigerator, cooling provisions in a natural way. A large black walnut tree grew near a huge flat rock that was the center of our play—I remember staining our hands with the black dye in the hulls as we cracked those walnuts.

Not all of my childhood was play. From an early age I was pressed into service as my dad's work partner. Outside of the summer season, guests dwindled, workers moved on or were busy elsewhere, and Dad took me along nearly everywhere he went. In the 1940s, a state forest ranger had to be jack-of-all-trades, something for which my dad was well suited. A ranger might have to be a plumber one moment, a cop the next, and "firewood-cutter-in-chief" all the time. Among the duties were campsite management, forest fire control, law enforcement, and game management. The work was often dangerous, including details to arrest well-armed poachers who were dismissive of laws and law enforcement. My dad first taught me to shoot by using a .22 to take out annoying woodchucks, and because I was really good at it, it wasn't long until I was leveraged into helping him with some of the more precarious ranger duties.

Such was my crash-course introduction to the responsibilities of manhood while I was still a boy. Dad extended such trust in many arenas. Among the best times was helping him on fire lookout; I loved being high up in the cabs of the fire towers or strapped into a spotting plane hired by the PDFW to scour the horizon for smoke. In the fire towers of the 1940s and '50s, communications were primitive and signaling others to the presence of a fire was difficult. I can still picture lining up a lightning strike on the large circular maps of the Osborne Fire Finder device, and, because of my lifelong proclivity for all things mathematical, I enjoyed doing calculations on the map to identify a fire's location.

My dad was a state fire warden in addition to being a forest ranger. We spent a lot of time on fire lines. As I grew older, I became well acquainted with the backpack Indian tanks that held about five gallons of water with a hose connected to the trombone-style telescoping hand pump. At an early age I became equally familiar with fire rakes, shovels, chainsaws, and other fire-fighting equipment.

My dad was a far more patient man in the woods than he was at home. I think he was most comfortable outdoors—he worked hard and enjoyed the work. In the depth of winter, restricted indoors or at home, he drank too much and often turned violent, but in the woods he was a patient teacher. He knew the names of plants and critters and he shared his knowledge. We studied maps, but he also taught me how to navigate the woods by reading terrain. In the fire towers he'd point out landmarks and help me see the natural topography of the forest. I learned to conclude where water flowed, where berries congregated, where game might hole up in the heat of the day or where they might sneak off in the height of hunting season. I learned game trails and knew danger spots where there were sudden cliff faces or dense, dangerous stands of shrubbery and rhododendron capable of hiding bears. I would accompany him as he walked boundary lines and I helped him search for lost children or hunters, situations that seemed to occur frequently.

My dad actively taught me skills that I needed to survive in the woods, but he also taught me about hard work, tenacity, and ingenuity. I watched him always, studying him as he thought his way through a problem or engineered some device that we needed. I saw how he used his authority in difficult circumstances, and how his quickness to anger usually got him in trouble and even weakened him. But I also watched him do the opposite, bringing people together to work out their differences or find mutually beneficial solutions.

When we lived at Hunters Range, most of the family was involved one way or another in harvesting timber from the eastern hardwood forests and transforming raw trees into usable wood at the family-owned sawmill. Dad not only increased the mill's efficiency, but he helped the family expand the business into more and more markets in western Pennsylvania and in bordering states. He was able to use his contacts through the state to negotiate better timber sales.

He thought in creative patterns and trusted his instincts. He taught me to do the same. I remember times when, after a long day of walking the forest boundary markers, my dad would turn to me and ask, "Do you know where you are?" I'd look around and acknowledge that I did, recognizing landmarks he'd been careful to point out on our many hikes. "Then I'll see you at home," he'd say, leaving me to navigate my way back. Some dog owners teach their dogs to swim by throwing them off a dock, a boulder, or a boat. That wasn't entirely the way my dad taught me to rely on my instincts while out in the woods, but he wasn't exactly afraid to test the success of the lessons he'd passed on. Secure in his teaching and confident in my abilities, he'd get in his truck and leave. I didn't mind. I felt at home in the woods. Navigating my way through the trees seemed instinctual to me. After all, when Dad was drunk or in a foul mood, I'd disappear into the woods with as much ease as I found my way home.

Of course, even boys raised in the woods have to grow up. The skills my father taught me in my childhood have served me throughout my life. Not just navigating or woodcraft or shooting, but confidence, determination, and an ability to stay level-headed no matter what was tossed my way. I don't know what I did to earn my dad's trust, but I was an eager student. So much of what my father taught me seemed entirely natural.

I am certain I would not have survived Vietnam were it not for my father's lessons in my youth. Because of nature of the missions I was assigned there, I frequently had to make my way back to secure areas from behind enemy lines, skirting patrols, and surviving what could be a lethal jungle. Deep in the jungles of Vietnam is where I felt most at home during my tour of duty, for even if their topography, flora, fauna, and weather were entirely new to me, they still felt like the woods and the places I had known and loved all my life. Sometimes passage back to safety took days of hiking. Typically, men on such missions lost weight or grew sickly during these long, dangerous treks. I put on weight, hunting as I moved and foraging edible fruits and plants that Vietnamese friends had taught me to identify.

To thrive in such a lethal place may seem odd to most, but I felt safer in the jungle than I did on firebases or in Da Nang's unpredictable streets and targeted command compounds. I suppose that's because I hunted and tracked game all my life. Early in my military career when I was training as a pilot, the Marines sent me to California to complete Survival, Evasion, Resistance, Escape (SERE) school in Pickle Meadows, which offered intensive training. This mountain survival school curriculum not only felt right up my alley but that proved vital to my ability to thrive during my tour in Vietnam. (Although I suppose I need to admit that, fed up with the imprisonment that was part of the "escape" portion of SERE school and inspired by a nearby forest fire, I set a fire of my own and used the chaos and the smoke to advance to the waypoint required to pass the course.)

In my forties I became a licensed outfitter and guide, taking clients on bear and elk hunts in Montana, a place that by then had become my second home. The freedom and beauty of the place made me remember my childhood in the backwaters of Pennsylvania, even if the sky was a lot bigger and the woods far less dense.

While my dad played the lead during my formative years, others had significant roles as well. When I was about four years old, my cousin Edie (formally named Edith Ann), who lived in Bethlehem, Pennsylvania, began to spend summers with our family. We were so close that I thought of her as a sister—still do, actually. From the day after school let out until the day before it started again in the fall, Edie and I spent most of our summers together, playing in the lake and the woods around the camp. Edie was not a very healthy child, and Bethlehem, a steel-producing town full of plants powered by coal, was extremely polluted, exacerbating Edie's health problems. She developed rheumatic fever at a young age, and we all feared for her, which was the reason she came to live with us in the fresh air of the Pocono Mountains. My mother became a second mother to Edie, and they shared a special relationship for the rest of my mother's life.

When we moved from Hunters Range to Promised Land, Edie came to live with us every summer until our adolescence, providing me a friend and a playmate. She was my partner in adventure; we spent our time boating, canoeing, fishing, and searching for arrowheads. We hunted snakes and squirrels. We found the most ordinary things to be great fun, like roasting potatoes in a can over the fire. And when a much older cousin, Ernie Bush (whom I loved and referred to as Uncle Ernie) returned from the Army after World War II with a parachute, Edie and I put it to a myriad of uses in our imaginative play.

If Edie was my "partner in crime," Uncle Ernie—who eventually became the chief geologist for the oil company Aramco—was my hero. Much to my father's chagrin, I even carried Ernie's photo in my wallet for several years as a boy. He loomed larger than life in my eyes. He lived the sorts of adventures to which I was naturally drawn—reaching such stature that he rode horses with the Shah of Iran and traveled frequently to Saudi Arabia. Hearing his stories from such adventures made me want to seek out my own.

Ernie lived in a beautiful house, once owned by Gifford Pinchot, where the floors were carpeted with impressive Persian rugs that he brought back from his travels. Uncle Ernie knew how to live and he knew how to fuel and encourage a child's dreams. He bought an out-of-service Jeep, and in it we tore around the back roads of the Pennsylvania mountains that we knew so well. He also bought a surplus glider, which was common and readily available after the war's end when they no longer served a purpose. He brought it to our place where Edie and I played in it for hours on end, pretending we were flying wartime missions. Besides real or imagined exploits in Jeeps and gliders, we also rode horses and ran cattle. We helped build boats and harvest fruit. With our extended family, childhood summers were filled with picking berries, collecting fruit, canning garden vegetables, butchering hogs, smoking ham and bacon, making scrapple. As playmates, we went coon hunting, swam in Lake Wallenpaupack, and cut bait for my fishermen uncles—in short, we enjoyed every manner of recreation the freedom of living in the mountains provided.

Uncle Ernie offered me an education of a different sort as well. My own parents were smart and hardworking, but they didn't have the chance to advance beyond high school degrees. Naturally, this limited their opportunities because there wasn't much economic prosperity in the rural places they had known all their lives. But because Uncle Ernie made his way to earn degrees from the University of Colorado and Colorado State University (then Colorado A & M), it was he who, when the time came, offered to pay my way through college. Ever proud and typically stubborn, my father refused his offer and said that he could take care of his own. Dad was smart and a good teacher in his own right, but he was probably jealous of Ernie's success in a world that was changing rapidly.

But what an education I received, learning to sustain our lives from the land. My home at the ranger station was large, with several extra bedrooms, so it became a kind of default boarding house where many of the workers lived with us—sometimes for months at a time. As a result, I lived among an "extended family" of other state forest employees, game wardens, contractors, and law enforcement officers. Many were experts in their respected fields, and I soaked up any knowledge they were patient enough to pass on. I had the chance to learn from engineers and firemen, biologists. and trade laborers. Such exposure, combined with my father's extensive knowledge of the woods, cars, engines, plumbing, electrical equipment, and construction, was crucial to my practical learning.

But my education wasn't restricted to lessons of the natural world or to the trades people earned by their hands. After our move from Saw Creek to Hunters Range, I was blessed to attend a one-room schoolhouse right next door to the ranger station, presided over by one Ann Cartwright. Miss. Cartwright had taught both my mother and my grandmother, and she was a truly remarkable woman. I attribute the foundation of my formal education to her abilities and her passion for teaching, for she provided me with the essential tools to learn. I vividly remember walking the 400 yards between school and my home on a path that led through rows of towering spruce trees. Reflecting a bit of my father's ingenuity, my cousin Arnold and I spent days and days hauling shale in our wagons from the roadsides to the path, creating a walkway to school that would allow us to keep our boots out of the mud.

There were nine of us in the one-room school, which was also home to the community's social clubs as well as the Audubon Society and 4-H. All nine of us students were members of these organizations where Ms. Cartwright taught us about good citizenship and animal husbandry—components of my education that would guide me throughout my life. The former school is now used as a community center for the Porter Township, and Anna Cartwright donated her farm and a huge adjoining parcel to the Boy Scouts of America. Now totaling 4,200 acres, the farm she owned is now at the center of the Resica Falls Scout Reservation. This is a fitting tribute to a remarkable woman who cared so much for the youth placed in her charge.

My own ingenuity can as likely be attributed to Anna Cartwright as to my father, for both showed an ability to build ideas from the ground up. For example, my first attempt as an entrepreneur happened when I was twelve or thirteen. I acquired a mimeograph and started my own newspaper, distributing it among campers who frequented the Promised Land campgrounds. I dubbed it "The Promised Land Weekly" and filled it with local news as its writer, editor, and publisher all at once. Whether they were just humoring an energetic adolescent, or they genuinely liked to catch up on local goings-on, campers and locals alike claimed to appreciate my efforts.

I liked to have my fingers in lots of things, which is how I occasionally discovered talents that I wouldn't have guessed I possessed. For example, during my junior year of high school I starred in the Pocono High School presentation of *Dino*. If we can believe the Strasburg newspaper's critic, he claimed he had "seldom seen … such depth and understanding" by an amateur. I suspect his charitable review was due to the involvement of film and television star Walter Burke, an actor I'd admired throughout my youth and who volunteered to help one of our teachers direct the show. Mr. Burke had a farm in Monroe County, so all the locals considered him their link to fame. I don't know if Mr. Burke was just being nice to a high school kid or if he really did see something in me, but he encouraged me to try my hand in Hollywood. I can't help but wonder what might have become of me if I'd followed such encouragement.

I suppose it was participation in amateur acting that helped give me the confidence to appear on *American Band Stand,* which filmed just down the road in Philadelphia. So, early on, I added Dick Clark's name next to Walter Burke's as famous people I'd met. That list grew later in life, as you'll learn. In fact, those encounters gave me the confidence that I drew on decades later when I gave speeches at conferences, appeared in television interviews, and testified before congressional subcommittees. That type of publicity came easily to me; maybe part of my nature is to show off a little, but I can also attribute such abilities to having good teachers at points in my life when it mattered most.

Early on, that push to try new things and then learn to excel at them was championed by my parents and my teachers. Miss. Cartwright's instruction largely paralleled the skills and philosophies that my parents emphasized. My father was a Mason, my mother a member of the Order of the Eastern Star, and I joined DeMolay as a teenager. All are respective parts of the Masonic Temple, which was founded on teachings of morality, charity, and obedience to the law of the land. Such an education dovetailed with the more elemental lessons my father focused on in the woods. While I became skilled in woodcraft, the real substance of my combined education—the one that has framed my life—stressed hard work and independence of thought and action.

When my dad received an offer to become the maintenance supervisor for the Golden Slipper Camp in 1952 (likely through my mother's finagling and certainly because of her contacts), he jumped on it. The Golden Slipper, another of the many camps, retreats, and resorts so common in the area, catered to kids from regional Jewish families who didn't have the good fortune I did to live among the

Poconos full time. Keeping such a sizable camp in prime operating shape, able to handle the hordes of kids it hosted every summer, was no small task and required year-round preparation.

At that point Dad officially left the ranger duties behind, but he continued doing many of the kinds of tasks he'd grown accustomed to while working for the state—and best of all, it kept me in my beloved mountains. That move also brought us closer to Stroudsburg and my grandmother, then eventually to the next phase of my education at what was then East Stroudsburg State Teachers College (now the East Stroudsburg campus of the University of Pennsylvania). There I focused on physics and mathematics, not exactly the same curriculum practiced in my classroom in the woods. However, my proclivity for those subjects points to a balance that has been important in my life between values and lessons I learned as a child and the factual, analytical approach I learned in the classroom. It also equipped me to differentiate between the physics demonstrated in the flight of a bullet and the courage to know when taking a shot is necessary (augmented by a moral compass to know when taking a shot is right). The roots of such a rounded and complex education were planted by my parents. The soil that enriched those roots was pure Pennsylvania dirt. That dirt, like my parents' fierce love, still courses through my veins.

Saddle Up

"He knew in that instant what he must do:
he must prove his courage to himself, and to
the others, or he could no longer live in their
midst." —Armstrong Sperry, *Call It Courage*

I can still hear screams of people drowning during a dark night in Pennsylvania floodwaters. I can picture the fatal injuries of Marines I served with in Vietnam. I vividly recall the tremble in my wife's voice as she told of facing a troubled seventeen-year-old hijacker. More vividly still, I remember the helplessness I felt at her bedside as she lay dying of cancer. There are many more such memories. So many tragedies. So much loss.

There's no explanation, at least none rooted in the earthly, for why I've been placed directly in the path of turmoil and tragedy with such regularity. Yet this has been the case from my earliest years. Perhaps it was the timing of my birth during the swift, exciting recovery period as our country emerged from the dark days of the Great Depression followed by the traumatic years of World War II. Everything and everyone seemed in a state of flux as the country tried to adapt to the dynamic change and sociological stresses of the new wartime economy. That's often been my feeling during my life—as though I had one step in a future that most people couldn't see coming.

Among my earliest memories were occasions with my father when we'd find dead bodies: victims of auto accidents, suicides or murders in cars along State Route 402 and other local highways. The roads around my childhood home seemed to attract tragic endings, whether for cosmic reasons or for the mundane reality of being a backwoods place two hours outside of New York City. Honestly, we made such discoveries with enough regularity that they didn't seem out of the ordinary to me. The reasons for these casualties weren't terribly distinct in my mind from the reasons that hunters, hikers, and campers became lost in the woods, or why some chose to take their lives within the boundaries of state parks and forest reserves. I've seen no shortage of people with bad judgement or a bad sense of direction. Eventually—and sadly—such people helped keep me gainfully employed.

My earliest memories are filled with floods and hurricanes and fires. When we lived at Saw Creek, our extended family—my father included—operated a sawmill. The mill's slag pile, which was practically a small mountain of tree limbs and trimmings from mill operations, caught fire. While it didn't harm the mill itself, that pile burned for months. A regular part of life for those at the mill was dousing the slow-burning fire with water. Doing so was a daily requirement for me, and I did it with a child's fascination for the other-worldly nature of fire—all that beauty and destruction wrapped up together.

That fire was more a nuisance, a fascination, and a hell of a lot of work than it was dangerous, but that wasn't always my experience. Working forest-fire lines with my dad exposed me to more than one close call. The worst I can remember was a time when Dad and I spotted a fire while it was still in its early stages, which made for some adrenaline. While we assessed the fire's perimeter, the wind abruptly changed direction and pushed the fire back to where we'd parked the car. It engulfed the car and melted its tires. Dad and I escaped by running into the creek.

I quickly learned that water itself took on dangerous qualities too. I think it was the same winter that my dad killed the horse to provide families with meat—it may have been during the trip to haul that meat—when a group of my relatives fell through a layer of ice. Because walking along the edges of the creek was easier than laboring through deeper snow on the nearby shore, everyone had taken to the ice. But, of course, we all know ice is thinner at the edges where the water is shallower and warmer. No one was at risk of drowning that day, but exposure to the brutal Pennsylvania cold while sopping wet is a recipe for disaster. I can also attest that seeing a whole group of your uncles and aunts crammed into a cabin and huddled around a fire in their all-togethers is good for a laugh. For better or worse, that's a memory that won't ever leave me.

Placed in such situations—even the funny ones—forced me to grow up fast. It was simply the hand I'd been dealt. More often than not, the circumstances weren't at all funny. One result is that I grew up to be a "get 'er done" kind of guy. I don't waffle over decisions. When something needs doing, I do it. This notion was reinforced dramatically in 1955 when I was fifteen and faced another incident involving water. Only this time there was too much of it.

That year, eastern Pennsylvania was hit back to back with the aftermaths of two massive storms that pounded the Atlantic seaboard—Hurricane Connie followed by Hurricane Diane. On August 18, after several days of endless and unprecedented rain, the Delaware and Lehigh Rivers overflowed their banks. Flooding was awful, cutting off entire sections of East Stroudsburg and affecting towns and villages throughout the Delaware drainage area. The river hit 43.7 feet near Easton, a record that has never been broken. The worst of the flooding near our home was focused on Brodhead Creek, normally a quiet fishing stream suddenly transformed into a raging river. Buildings, boulders, and trees from upstream were bulldozed by the moving water, forcing debris to pile up against a bridge over the Brodhead and forming a spontaneous dam. The debris included a number of railroad cars wedged under the bridge. When the bridge finally gave way to pressure, the makeshift dam burst, releasing a wall of water into the valley. Survivors described this monstrous, unforgiving water wall as reaching forty feet tall.

On that day we had gone down off the mountain to visit my Uncle Miller at Camp William Penn, a summer camp sponsored by the city of Philadelphia and close to Grandmother Miller's in Monroe County. It started to rain about noon, developing into a heavy rain that increased dramatically hour by hour without a break. My dad, watching the worsening conditions with worry, decided we'd better head home to Promised Land while we were still able. We proceeded over Snow Hill Road toward Creek Road which paralleled Brodhead Creek. Snow Hill Road was beginning to wash out, developing deep, surging gullies of muddy water on both sides. The road had become nearly impassable. Once we finally neared the paved Creek Road, we could see that it was entirely flooded.

Creek Road looked like a giant lake. Dad had me walk in the headlights ahead of the car so that we had some hope of knowing where the road surface was and gauging the water's depth. Rain continued in a torrential downpour and the sky was dark as ink. As water rose higher up my legs and I encountered entire trees floating across the road, we turned around and headed in the opposite direction—but by then the road was completely washed out. We turned around again and headed back toward Snow Hill but the water continued to get deeper. Pressing on in any direction was hopeless, but Dad was convinced that if we stayed were we were we'd be swept away so he steered the car up a muddy, primitive track into the woods where he knew there was higher ground. We abandoned the car there. Having to do so really bothered my mom because it was the first new car my parents had ever owned, a 1953 Chevy. She'd scrimped and saved from her job at the tire shop to be able to buy it, and it was her pride and joy.

We were close to a small resort named Rock Ledge Manor. It was no longer in operation, but we made the drenching walk through the downpour to the back of the building where we could jimmy a lock. We spent that night in a pitch-dark room, listening to screams of people caught in the nearby floodwaters. Even now, more than sixty years later, I can still hear the horrible sound of those poor people screaming.

The rain stopped before daylight, and with the sunrise we were faced with a startling disaster. Cabins from a nearby summer camp had literally washed away and were broken into pieces, jammed up like corks among the skeletal remains of bridges. People clung to trees and detached sections of roofs. We encountered a number of people gathered at the water's edge where they could see the bodies of family members but couldn't reach them due to the persistent high water. Many of the bodies had been stripped of their shoes and clothes. Surviving trees protruding from the floodwaters were littered with clothing reduced to rags along with saturated, ripped curtains and the battered remains of furniture. Little Brodhead Creek had turned into a swirling, deadly lake in the wake of the flood that had descended through its narrow channel. Typical of mountain floods, the water was swift moving and aggressive, leaving a once-familiar place hardly recognizable.

Knowing that passage by car would be impossible, we set out for Promised Land on foot. What we couldn't know was that we wouldn't see our car again for over a month because so much infrastructure had been destroyed. Our trip home, about twenty-five miles away, took all day even though we hitched rides on passable sections of roads. There was no power. Phone lines were down. Bridges were washed out. Houses were demolished and people were in shock. Later I learned that my high school, like most of the town where it was located, had flooded. I didn't return to school for months because of the damage. That day we lent a hand where we could, rescuing survivors from flooded cabins. We crossed streams in small boats that were roped back and forth by locals just as though we'd returned to the hand-powered ferries of a century before.

Evacuation was a serious priority. We had several hundred stranded campers at three major camping areas in Promised Land. We had to get food to them, so we created a temporary bridge by cutting trees and breaking into the old Civilian Conservation Corps storage buildings for lumber and materials. While we were able to help those campers under our charge at Promised Land, others elsewhere had not fared as well. Ultimately, we learned that at least seventy people had been killed in the floods caused by Hurricanes Connie and Diane. Thirty-seven of those deaths occurred at the camp near Rock Ledge Manor where we'd holed up that night.

I will never know how we escaped unscathed from the epicenter of the storm's deadly rage. That sort of luck has been a common pattern in my life—to be placed close to mayhem and yet to survive. Violence and danger have not been strangers to me, even in life's moments of relative "normalcy" and calm.

In the same moment that I feel sympathy during the tragedies of others and try to protect them from harm, I'm also fascinated by tense life-or-death situations. I've always been intrigued by the emotional extremes of events like births, deaths, fires, floods, and pestilence. There's an infectious energy in being near such raw moments of uncertainty. As I told an interviewer forty-five years later upon my retirement from Northwest Airlines, "Smoke and fire is my middle name." I've always thrived at the center of the action.

The happenchance nature of my life often conspired with my dad's foolhardy character to make sure I saw plenty more moments of unusual drama. Because the ranger station at Promised Land served as the hub of all activity including law enforcement actions, I was constantly exposed to many of life's dramatic scenes. It was the center of trauma and the chief meeting place for folks around the area.

This meant that I frequently encountered people when they were at their worst. Just as there was no shortage of tragedy in the

Pennsylvania mountains of my youth, there was no shortage of miscreants either. I suppose that's true anywhere, but it felt particularly true in our neck of the woods. We regularly found evidence of poachers and sometimes we encountered the poachers themselves. Part of the daily reality of a forest ranger is to interact with well-armed individuals who've already proven to be dismissive of laws. Not only did a forest ranger often work alone, he might also be the only authority within an hour's reach or more. Arresting professional poachers was dangerous business especially since they seldom worked alone. On the occasions when my dad *did* have a partner, his partner was a mere boy—me. More than once when I was growing up, I found myself holding a loaded weapon on poachers or game violators while my dad made an arrest. We rehearsed scenarios that positioned me where I'd be able to shoot those he was arresting without endangering him. His most emphatic piece of advice in these situations was: "Whatever happens, don't shoot *me*."

I remember one instance when a disgruntled, slightly amused poacher said to my dad, "Well, you're all by yourself. What are you going to do?"

"No, I'm not," my dad responded. "I've got my son."

"Well, he's just a little boy. What's he going to do? Shoot us? That gun's bigger than him."

My dad replied, "I wouldn't recommend you test him. I've never seen him miss."

The one time I recall having to prove my dad right didn't come while Dad was in an official capacity, but rather at home and in front of my mom. I was visiting home for the weekend. I'd graduated from East Stroudsburg State University the previous year and had taken a teaching position in Stroudsburg, where I lived with my grandmother, as I 'd done while in college. I found teaching unsatisfying, and was restless. My mom woke me in the middle of the night, saying, "I think someone's stealing your car."

Now, I loved my car. I had worked hard to earn enough to buy it. It was a 1962 Chevy Impala SS entirely modified by hand by a regional racing team. It would go 156 miles per hour, powered by a 327-cubic inch, 300 horse-power engine. People all knew my car. And they knew me.

It was summertime. The windows were open. We lived in an old rural farmhouse not too far from the Golden Slipper Camp. When my mom woke me up I grabbed the Colt .44 single action that was hanging on my bed, but Dad told me he'd take the Colt and I should get the shotgun instead. I did as he said and loaded it with shells that we always kept in the kitchen drawer. My dad was the first outside. We recognized the two guys, who were about my age—James Motts and Robert Cayes, known in the area as troublemakers. They were your standard malcontents, a sort who weren't unusual in the backwoods of Pennsylvania. I'd seen them around Johnson's Diner where I'd hang out with friends when I was home. It wasn't clear if they were trying to steal my car or nab the wheels off of it. They later claimed that the whole incident was nothing more than a practical joke, but I knew better. Most likely they were drunk. My dad, knowing their nature, disarmed them, making them place their weapons on the ground. When Dad moved to put them in flex cuffs and detain them for the sheriff, they went for their weapons so he shouted "Shoot 'em!" I didn't hesitate. I hit Motts with a round of birdshot.

Dad cuffed them while Motts lay bleeding and stunned in the gravel driveway of our farmhouse. I had meant to stun them, not kill them, and I'd winged Motts in the arm. Dad said we needed to get him medical attention. Using a rug and a quilt in the trunk, we put the wounded thieves in the back seat of the car and took Motts to Dr. Tether, our only local physician. He took a look, then told us he'd patch him up as best he could but that we needed to take them on to the hospital. My dad used Dr. Tether's phone to call the hospital and tell them we were coming. "You really let the air out of him," the doctor said to me as we departed.

Now, while they were the sort who were always in trouble and who vowed they'd get even with me for letting loose with birdshot, the truth was I couldn't claim to be a whole lot better than them. Though I was class president in high school and a good student in college, I was something of a trouble maker. Nowadays I like to tell people that I am a bastard by birth, son of a bitch by nature, and a gentleman by an act of Congress. None of that is quite literally true, but in my teens and twenties I was certainly capable of being a sort of firebrand. I had a nose for fights, I liked to drive fast, and I helped pay for college by selling deer meat—a hell of a lot of deer meat—to local diners. I would never think of stealing someone's car, but I wasn't sorry for defending my property by shooting those who would. And I wasn't the least bit afraid of Motts' and Cayes' threat to "get even"—I've never been one to be intimidated. Those who have tried have been sorry for it. I can't argue that while sensible people run from gunfire, I've always been the sort to run towards it.

Maybe it was my own penchant for trouble and my family's worry that I'd become like the lowlifes who tried to steal from me, or maybe it was concern that the likes of Motts and Cayes might truly seek retribution from me, but knowing I was dissatisfied teaching, my folks began encouraging me to enlist and to get out of Pennsylvania.

Though I had a 1-S deferment during college, I knew that I'd have a low draft number afterward and would likely end up in the Army when all I really wanted to do was fly jets. Rather than wait for my draft number to come up, I enlisted with the Marines—intent on controlling my fate and becoming an officer and a pilot. I attended Officer Candidate School in Quantico, Virginia, and then I qualified to attend Aviation Officer Candidate School in Pensacola, Florida. While there I was named student of the week, student of the month, and then finished at the top of my class during rigorous training in the A-4 Skyhawk. Three officer candidates were selected from our class—two went on to pilot helicopters, and I got my wish to fly jets.

During carrier flight training on board the USS Lexington, I survived a midair collision with another attack fighter. Let me tell you, if you're someone who likes action raw and up close, having to punch out of an A-4 canopy will do it. In another incident, during a cross-country training flight to California, I had two pressure losses at 35,000 feet altitude and lost all navigational aids on the way out all while encountering bad weather. Such was the nature of aircraft, a thing I learned well enough flying in Vietnam two years later.

The Marines trained me well and I was placed in a number of specialized, intensive courses—each aimed at teaching me how to survive dogfights and, if shot down, how to avoid detection and capture. These were skills I put to the test regularly. I'd been trained on a number of different aircraft, but there wasn't a lot of call for Marine jet pilots (the Air Force and Navy had those assignments sewn up). Instead, we were needed in helicopters. I flew some of those during my first month in Vietnam before ending up with the U-10 Helio Courier, dropping psychological operations (PSYOP) leaflets on the enemy and blaring messages to them from loudspeakers. We referred to the Helio Courier as a "bullshit bomber" due to the nature of our missions. As a tactic of psychological warfare, we dropped bullshit in the form of leaflets instead of bombs, propaganda aimed at encouraging enemy combatants to changes sides. At the outset of my time with PSYOPs, I'd have said you were crazy if you believed such missions had any meaning. It's ironic that I, someone who thought I'd only engage the enemy in dogfights and close air support strafes, eventually spent most of my tour of duty training and fighting alongside those former enemies—individuals who acted on our "bullshit" leaflets.

The U-10 was a remarkably nimble little plane, but when people are shooting at you, it's slow as molasses. It could fly low and maneuver well. It was designed to land on runways shoveled by farmers without breaking apart, making it a big hit with the CIA, as I soon discovered. Flying a U-10, you quickly learned to expect small-arms fire to riddle your wings and fuselage, and you flew with your butt puckered waiting for a slug to come through the seat cushion.

When it came to raw human drama, Vietnam had it in spades. If I wasn't flying, or plunging deep into the jungle on missions, or operating out on Hill 55 in support of special operations forces, I was at headquarters in Da Nang. That coastal city had become pretty westernized by then, and it was—like the rest of the country during wartime—entirely unpredictable. We never knew if the Viet Cong were hiding among the local population, or, for that matter, if they'd infiltrated civilian workers hired on the base. I quickly learned to carry a Colt .45 everywhere I went. And I mean everywhere, including sleeping with it under my pillow and taking it to the shitter. Once you get used to it, a .45 is just about as comforting as a teddy bear.

It was common for nightly mortar attacks and grenades to launch over the fence that served as a thin perimeter between our base and the wild and wooly streets of Da Nang. On one particularly memorable night, the Viet Cong managed to get some of their guys onto a Vietnamese work crew that was building a new barracks next to the one where I bunked. At about 0400 they poured ten gallons of gas onto a brand-new white truck that was parked thirty feet from where I was sleeping, and then they torched the thing. You can't imagine the sound of the WHOOSH that erupted when that gas tank blew. Along with the few other guys sleeping in the barracks I managed to get out before the fire reached our wooden building, but the flames at the truck were thirty feet high. It's a good thing I slept with my gun, because somebody had to dispatch the little bastards who tried to kill us. My fellow Marines and I took care of those unfortunate souls, but there always seemed to be more where they came from.

When a gook got killed by Marines in Vietnam, he really got killed. I saw German Shepherds burst through fences and rip them to shreds. I witnessed tanks drive over men on bicycles. I watched night skies light up with napalm as a jungle filled with Viet Cong was incinerated. Most of the time you didn't see the enemy until they were killed. It was full-scale guerrilla war and counterinsurgency, practically before those words were part of our vocabulary. The bad "guy" coming to kill us might actually have been a woman or a grandfather or an adolescent, and we might have had chow with that person only thirty minutes before.

We didn't always know where to look for the enemy. It could be quiet as a Pennsylvania winter day after a big dump of snow (though it never felt like any Pennsylvania winter, with temperatures that often climbed over 120 degrees), and then at night it could feel like the gates of hell had opened. One night a group of Viet Cong sappers swam in from a fishing boat and blew up one of our helipads along with several copters. Our firefight to take out the insurgents lasted for more than three hours.

Firefights inside the compound were always the worst because you never knew who was doing the shooting. They nearly always came in the dark and too often some of the men began shooting indiscriminately, so comrades could be every bit as dangerous as the enemy. When people are shooting *at* shadows inside a compound *from* inside a compound, it gets pretty hairy. Too often some of the good guys got plugged in the process.

I remember one incident demonstrating how unpredictable Da Nang was—it happened when gunfire erupted within the fence. A swab (one of our Navy brethren) stole one of our Jeeps, got drunk, and wrecked it behind the building where I slept. Intoxicated by booze and by whatever injustice he felt the government had committed by placing him in the war, or fueled by a Dear John letter, he started spraying bullets. The whole compound went wild thinking the Viet Cong had gotten through the gate. Needless to say, that sailor didn't last long in the crossfire. A lieutenant was hit with fragments from a grenade that someone threw. In a way, that type of chaos was typical. On base at Da Nang, everyone just waited for something to happen and we were all armed to the teeth. When an excuse to cut loose came along, I guess a lot of people got a little overanxious. Too bad about the swab.

Of course, there were also large-scale firefights, missions behind enemy lines, tunnels to blow and villages to sweep among other scary, nearly daily events that occurred throughout my thirteen months in-country. At any rate, it didn't take long to realize that I'd entered a place where danger was everywhere and often invisible. Far from the backwoods of my sweet old Poconos, I now lived in a place where, more often than not, I fell asleep to the sound of mortars and gunfire. Something truly frightening happened nearly every day. Yet I'd be lying if I didn't admit that a part of me enjoyed the rush of those adrenaline spikes. The thrill of opening up the throttle on a combat jet wasn't really so different from putting the pedal to the floor in my Impala. When you're regularly in the company of death, you damn sure know when you're alive.

If foreordained timing determined that I'd serve my country during the thick of the Vietnam years, it also placed me in a series of unusual events upon my return. And here I'm talking about something more than the general upheaval of our country so affected by change that it hardly seemed identifiable. I had entered the Marines wanting to fly jets, and I'd been intentional during my time there to ensure that I might be in the best position to fly commercial airliners once I was discharged from the military. I'd even refused two purple hearts due to worry that they might harm my medical standing for gaining a pilot's license for one of the airlines. I'd also thought long and hard about accepting offers from the State Department to stay on in Vietnam and continue the work to which I'd become dedicated—although, in official-speak at least, I'd be in a civilian capacity. If I hadn't had a wife and a child waiting for me back home, that offer, like the money promised to go along with it, would have been very tempting. But it also would have delayed a potential flight career, and a delay could mean missing out entirely. I'd always been driven. It felt like it was time to get on with my life. Besides, I knew I'd been lucky to reach my DEROS (Date of Expected Return from Overseas) alive and with all my limbs. Yet just as I'd had the "fortune" to be born into an age that landed me in a war, I'd come home to an airline industry deep in the quagmire of a threat barely registered in earlier years: airplane hijackings.

I began my commercial career with what was then Northwest Orient Airlines in late 1967. It may be hard to fathom today, but between May 1961 and the end of 1972 there were 159 hijackings in American airspace or aboard American aircraft. The very worst came in a five-year period starting in 1968 when hijackers seized commercial jets at a rate of nearly once a week. But to a member of a flight crew tasked with getting passengers safely to their business meetings or family vacations, it felt like there was a hijacking every day. Before those five years were over, I'd be in the thick of the defense against what came to be known as "skyjacking" in ways that felt like the stuff of suspense novels. Suffice it to say, I became what you might call "intimate" with disturbed lunatics who thought threatening to kill innocent people was either an expedient way to wrangle ransom money, or an ideal platform to herald a misguided political cause.

Briefcases, paper bags, cardboard boxes, carry-on luggage—all of these ordinary items had been used to threaten flight crews as containers of explosive devices. Some items were merely decoys, some were empty threats, and some proved to be the real deal. Telling the difference became part of my FBI training, but for a decade or more the shear menace of such a threatening device was enough to make airlines comply with hijacker demands without questioning the veracity of their threats. In the early years, nearly all of these demands involved rerouting the aircraft to Havana, either with hijacker claims of solidarity with Cuban citizens or by Cubans themselves seeking return to their homeland after their revolution. Over time the demands grew more politically diverse and more extravagant—flights to North Vietnam in protest of the war or to the Middle East in support of the Palestinian Liberation Front. Many became outright cash grabs.

For years the airlines complied with all demands—accepting compliance as a way to protect passengers and to avoid a public relations catastrophe that would result from any incident where passengers were injured or killed. In hijackings with Cuba as the final destination, an airline's cost would typically be little more than a nominal fee to the Cuban government for release of the airplane once the hijackers were handed over to Cuban authorities (who ironically jailed the hijackers, usually for life, rather than award them a hero's welcome). As circumstances shifted and hijackers became more brazen, more violence ensued (accidental and otherwise).

Increasingly, both the airlines and the FBI took a more zealous approach to putting a rapid end to hijack attempts. The Bureau was on a steep learning curve with a class of criminal behavior that fell largely outside their previous experience. As time went on, the FBI became far more aggressive in utilizing snipers, aircraft assault teams, aircraft disablement, and other responses to confront hijackers. As agents grew bolder in their response and airlines began, reluctantly and sporadically, to screen passengers and use limited security protocols, the numbers of hijackings that occurred in the late 1960s and early '70s slowed substantially. Most would-be hijackers began to realize that the odds were stacked against them, for a typical hijacking now ended with the hijacker's death or arrest.

I'll share one story that illustrates my involvement in what would become the fight against such criminal activity and that captures the nature of the era. My contributions to counterterrorism would ultimately guide much of my professional life for decades as the industry came to understand that it was a prime target both for the mentally disturbed and for the terrorist seeking martyrdom.

In the early 1980s, acting in a role I'd taken on nearly a decade before that led to intensive training in counterterrorism, explosive device retrieval, and close combat techniques by the FBI, I was summoned to Chicago O'Hare International Airport. The FBI had doubled the program Operation Switch. A troubled young man had seized control of a Northwest Airlines flight. This psychiatric patient claimed to have a bomb in a bag on his lap, a scenario that had become all too common. Assessing the situation, the first thing I did was ask the pilot to turn the plane's air conditioning system to its coldest setting and run the fans. I waited a good while before boarding the aircraft, and then, rather than camouflage my identity in the guise of an aircraft mechanic (among the deceptions we regularly applied in such incidents) or use other subterfuge, I appeared in Chicago as the relief pilot, ready to take the hijacker on his long-haul diversion. Upon entering the aircraft, I sat next to the hijacker and calmed him by assuring him that I was prepared to be compliant. I talked with him, working to gain his trust. While, by nature, I'm quicker to employ the trigger than diplomacy, I'm also capable—or so I'm told—of being charming. I certainly had some experience in trying to win over the enemy. Indeed, that was my primary job in Vietnam.

In this case, I succeeded in getting the hijacker to relax a bit and accept that I was going to play my part in getting him to his destination. I complained about the how cold the airplane was and told him that he looked cold as well. When I asked if he'd like me to get him a blanket and he accepted, I saw my chance. When he reached to take the blanket from me, I pounced. I moved the bag allegedly containing a bomb to the empty seat beside him and then pinned him to his seat with all my weight. Other agents quickly helped subdue him. To all of our relief, the bag was empty. The split second that transpired as I made my move on the hijacker, eying his bag all the while, seemed to last a lifetime. That's the nature of fear-filled situations. You nearly hold your breath waiting for the explosion, waiting for the sniper's bullet, waiting for the incoming shell. In those moments you run away or you take action.

My core personality trait is to take action, and that instinct guides my philosophical beliefs about people and about policy as well. While others hemmed and hawed about meeting terrorist demands, I advocated for policies of taking immediate action. When airline corporations thought they would lose passengers if they implemented any kind of security screening, I stood firm in the belief that there were proactive means to filter the bad guys from the good guys that wouldn't be overly disruptive. While bureaucrats and airline marketing heads tried to appear serious about the importance of security when they were really protecting their wallets, I argued that those given the responsibility for transporting passengers also needed to be provided the tools and training required to remove any threat. I spent many years and wore out a lot of shoe leather advocating for those beliefs.

Why have I remained so firm in my convictions throughout a long career in airline security? Well, likely because I've been exposed to those moments that called for instant action and intervention nearly all of my life. You have to be present in the face of imminent danger to know how you'll react. I'm not proud of the fact that I predicted the kind of terror our country faced on September 11—even a decade or more before that awful day arrived—but because I've lived through volatile circumstances, I've learned to expect the unexpected and to see the vulnerabilities in any given system.

Sometimes, of course, particularly if you're an adrenaline junkie, danger arrives for stupid reasons rather than noble ones when you're just trying to have a little fun. I do like to experiment. Old family friends, witnesses to my curiosity, saw how high the remains of a stubborn tree stump would blow when I applied a stick of dynamite to it. (The answer, if you care to know, was high enough to send it over the roof of the house.) Speaking of dynamite, my daughters can explain how effectively a stick of it will speed up a slow day of fishing.

And sometimes my favorite activities all combine into one escapade. I remember a trip to Montana back before I took up residence there. It was probably during a hunting trip if I had to hazard a guess. I'd flown in with a pilot friend, and we'd rented a car. It was long after dark, and we'd stopped to buy some beer. We didn't have a cooler, so we poured ice into the back seat. (Of course, since we'd had a long day, we put some of that beer to good use.) Somewhere along our route I spotted a coyote loping along in the prairie. Now, as a general rule I believe that I'm duty bound to remove coyotes from the landscape. That means you've got to catch up with the bastards first— they are evasive creatures. I've been accused of having nine lives. I'm more than certain that most coyotes lead at least that many.

We'd rented a sedan, not ideal for coyote hunting, but that's what we had. I turned off the road and tried to keep the coyote in my headlights. Did I mention that it was dark? My philosophy is that if you lack four-wheel drive, momentum helps. We had a heck of a good time trying to chase that fellow down. In case you haven't experienced it for yourself, let me inform you that the prairie isn't nearly as flat as it looks from an airplane cockpit—or from a well-paved road for that matter. It turns out you can get a rental car airborne and it'll still hold together. Well, sort of. By the time we returned it to the agency, it would only go in one gear: reverse.

As much fun as things like driving fast can be, sometimes—as was the case in a lot of the stories I've shared, regularly exposing myself to hazards resulted in situations that didn't always plaster a smile on my face. And I can attest that living dangerously with such regularity doesn't remove fear. The presence of fear when encountering life-or-death circumstances is inevitable. Some will stare down that fear and take action regardless of its presence. Learning to face the things that scare us most was precisely the message of my favorite childhood book, *Call it Courage,* by Armstrong Sperry.

Our culture needs courageous people. We need the firefighters who labored under the weight of their equipment as they climbed the stairs of the World Trade Center while terrified civilians streamed down towards safety. We need the soldiers who turn toward enemy fire when their natural instincts tell them to turn away. We need pilots and flight attendants dedicated to protecting their passengers when their airplanes are threatened. I don't consider myself particularly brave, but I've always been willing to saddle up and face the unknown. After all, someone has got to do it.

Deadeye

The first life I ever took, aside from those of numerous woodchucks (which my dad believed made excellent target practice for a boy), was that of my dog. Her name was Fawn, and she was a registered Cocker Spaniel that my parents had given me from one of the litters they routinely bred. She was my constant companion and my first real love, but she'd fallen ill with distemper. My dad explained that distemper was frequently fatal and definitely debilitating and painful. Handing me a .22 Harrington & Richardson 999, he asked, "Are you going to let her suffer?"

As much as I didn't want to kill her, I knew it was the humane thing to do. I could see the pain she was in. She was no longer the dog I had known. I took her out behind the house and ended her misery. I was probably seven or eight years old.

Having to kill my dog was something that I never forgot. It left a scar. Yet scars can be beneficial things, for they offer reminders. They can teach lessons as well, in this case not just about the power of a weapon but about the grave circumstances when a person must choose to use it. I learned early on that guns can be used as a means to assault others to force them to do your bidding, or they can be used to protect those who cannot defend themselves. To use a steady hand in order to keep innocent people from harm is a noble act, one that justifies utilizing the tremendous power of a firearm. And sometimes, as in Fawn's condition, a gun becomes a tool of mercy.

I may've participated in far too many fistfights in my life, and I probably enjoyed them too much, but I've never been a bully. On the other hand, I've encountered more than my share of them. Too often they've been armed. Sometimes a gun becomes a necessary instrument, and sometimes mercy comes at relieving the world of someone with the intent to do harm.

Such lessons about guns and their power were given to me early in my life. As I suggested in the foreword, my ability to shoot with accuracy and to take a shot when circumstances called for it is what set much of my career in motion. My ability to shoot straight, in more than one use of the phrase, opened a lot of doors for me. Sometimes directly and sometimes indirectly, my reputation with a weapon grew and began to precede me. Some who understood the character required for proficiency in shooting saw my potential to accomplish things far beyond what a well-placed bullet could.

I grew up in a gun culture, one where I was taught from the outset that carrying a weapon was a tremendous responsibility. Guns were an important part of our life at the ranger stations. They were necessary tools of both ranger law enforcement and wildlife management. In my family, we spent a lot of time practicing gun safety and learning how to shoot properly. Most of our meat, unless we raised it, came from hunting. We were a hunting family through and through. Fall—and with it, hunting season—was and remains my favorite time of year.

From my youth, guns simply felt natural in my hand, an extension of myself. I enjoyed the long process of trying to master efficiency and accuracy in its use. Other boys I knew were interested in baseball and football. I only wanted to shoot. I've taught a lot of people to shoot in the years since. Some take to it easily and quickly. Others never do. I do believe there's something to the notion of natural ability and I was blessed with it. Shooting with accuracy requires careful body position that establishes balance. It requires control over your breathing and control over your mind. To be a good shooter, you learn to be disciplined. To hunt with repeated success, you've got to be able to understand distance and speed and velocity well enough to know how and when to lead your target and how to accommodate for bullet drop at long distances. When sniping, you have to learn to incorporate windspeed—the world gets reduced to that crosshair.

My mind is naturally mathematical, so I come to these calculations naturally and nearly instantaneously. Like most things in life, if you do enough of something, you not only become good at it but you also don't have to really think about it. I've done so much shooting for so many years that I don't think a lot about the basics, and so my body does most of the work for me. I guess you could say that over time I learned to "think" the bullet into the target.

More than just loving to shoot from the time I was a little kid, I wanted to know all about guns—how they were made and why they are constructed and designed the way they are. I wanted to understand their materials and the science of how they worked. I enjoyed learning about their history and their unique variations and modifications. By the time I was a teenager, I'd moved well beyond firing and cleaning weapons and began working on them. I learned that gunsmithing was in equal measure a science and an art. Working on the mechanics of a weapon suited my nature and my ability to use my hands, a trait I valued whether in helping build or repair something around the camp, butchering an animal, or repairing a car. I like the feel of grease on my fingers. I love the smell of gun oil. I spent so many hours working on guns that gun oil is the scent my children associate with me. I enjoy the knowledge of how a tool is designed. And from the beginning, I readily understood that a gun was a tool—one that could be used for good or bad based entirely on the intentions of its user.

From early childhood on, I learned that a carefully cared-for gun could save my ass. This lesson was more than reinforced during my college years when I drudged through web-like, shadowy mazes of rhododendrons in search of wounded black bears. Rhododendrons can reach the height of a room and are so invasive that sometimes it seems that they've grown limbs and are intent on entombing the unwary. Hunting bears is tricky business itself; I learned quickly just how smart a bear is. You can turn from hunter to prey quicker than a girl will slap your face if you comment on her best friend's looks. When you crawl into the dark and thorny undergrowth of a Pennsylvania forest, following the blood trail of an animal that can rip your chest open with one swipe, you want a weapon that's dependable and relatively portable—a weapon that comes to shooting position rapidly and possesses good firepower. It's crucial to be able to shoot fast and shoot accurately. And you've got to have stopping power. I favored a .338 Winchester Magnum as my cartridge of choice when a bear was on the other end. Tracking bears will definitely keep your heart racing (and, I might add, it was pretty damn good training down the road, both for stalking Viet Cong and for reacting encountering hijackers).

A gun, managed with intelligence, could also be a lot of fun. As I was growing up, shooting was a regular family activity at Grandmother Miller's, especially during holidays and large family get-togethers. Many of my uncles and other relatives who'd returned from the war brought home several fine examples of European firearms. These were added to the arsenal of rifles and pistols amassed by the family and routinely tested on targets attached to a large tree at my grandmother's place. Aficionados all, we held competitions and practices, unleashing tons of ammunition. In the process, we eventually reduced that tree, once three feet in diameter, to a stump. Although I've had my share of fishing success, I suspect it's the efficiency of a firearm that makes me choose hunting over fishing—if I were forced to choose, that is. Of course, in the right circumstance, a "shotgun fishing pole" could do the trick.

I eventually learned that being good with a gun could also prove profitable. I joined the high school shooting team and loved the chance to compete at something I not only enjoyed but at which I excelled. Of course, my high school only had sixteen kids and most of them were girls, so to a large extent I *was* the shooting team. In high school and college, I frequently diversified the meat offerings at our dinner table because turkeys and hams and roasts were often the prizes offered at shooting competitions. This was an age in which the nature of the competition—not unlike the one depicted in the Gary Cooper film *Sergent York*—was to walk sixty paces, turn, and fire at a turkey's head sticking out of a protective cage. If the shooter was skilled and fast enough, it was a clean kill. A successful shot could win you the rest of the turkey.

By college, my reputation for shooting helped to land me a job with Tom McCool and the McCool Gun Company. I worked for the company from the age of sixteen all through my college years. Tom McCool, a longtime friend of my mother's, was an outstanding gunsmith, and people throughout our area turned to him to restore antique weapons, rebore rifles, build custom guns, and sell ammo. He catered to a number of wealthy customers. His gun range was a gathering place, one where lots of locals went to sight their weapons. More than that, it was a lucrative business venture in satisfying folks' hunger for entertainment during the summer season. McCool had contracts with a number of area resorts and summer camps; their guests were bussed to the McCool Company shooting range to experience the "outdoor life" and try their hand at shooting a variety of weapons, including Winchester .22 pumps, M1 rifles, M1 carbines, .45 1911 pistols, and a Remington semi-automatic 12-gauge shotgun as well as novelty guns which were particularly good for photo opportunities. Customers paid by the round, and once some of them got the taste of shooting they expended a hell of a lot of rounds. We'd painted metal targets that went out two hundred yards at twenty-five-yard increments, and novice shooters loved the sound of the "ping" when they successfully hit a target.

To provide a bit of atmosphere and excitement, Tom and Kate McCool fashioned up a bit of mountain drama by staging a sharpshooting display which featured a certain local youth known for his prowess at pulling a trigger. I've never exactly been the shy sort; some have accused me of enjoying being the center of attention. I loved putting on shows where I could demonstrate any number of trick shots. Perhaps Walter Burke had been onto something after my high school stage debut and I could have made it in Hollywood. At McCool's I'd grab five clay pigeons, throw them up in the air, and hit them all with five rounds, western style. Only I used an old Army-issue .45, which made a terrific noise and increased the challenge because it could be a difficult gun to control. I'd play to the spectators, choosing from the crowd a pretty lady wearing a big diamond ring, and then I'd sight through the diamond's refraction to make a trick shot. I'd shoot on the run and shoot behind my back. I'd shoot left-handed and shoot at moving targets. The whole range was set up against a hillside, and some targets would make noise or set off little explosions upon impact. Sometimes I'd ding a metal plate to produce a ricochet. The crowd loved it.

The McCools even had a small French cannon that they'd shoot off to end the performance; funny how we always managed to pick some pretty young thing to light its fuse. The area where shooters lined up to try their luck at targets was under cover so that the range could remain open in inclement weather, and when that cannon was fired with black powder, smoke filled the range and a boom echoed throughout. The crowds got pretty excited and they were willing to empty their pockets for the chance to make some noise themselves.

The McCools were outstanding people, and Tom taught me a great deal about gunsmithing as well as entertaining. It was there that I began to learn skills I'd apply for many years (minus the trick shooting, pretty girls, and cannon fire), eventually owning my own gunsmithing business. I even lived with the McCools during my summers in college so that I could continue to learn from Tom, work at the range as needed, and be closer to Stroudsburg and my part-time job at American Stores. By then my dad's drinking had worsened, and the McCools offered a refuge from his unpredictable moods.

In 1962 I had the tremendous opportunity to take my shooting skills to the national rifle matches at historic Camp Perry, Ohio. Camp Perry is located on the shore of Lake Erie near Port Clinton, Ohio, and has hosted national matches as well as military shooting competitions and training since 1907. There I got to bunk in former WWII prisoner-of-war huts and shoot on all four of the ranges named for Medal of Honor recipients Viale, Young, Petrarca, and Rodriguez. We attended the small-arms firing course run by the Army Infantry School, ate in the mess hall, and enjoyed the camaraderie of other skilled shooters. Among the trainers at Camp Perry I met Carlos Hathcock, who would go on to become the most famous sniper of the Vietnam War. During the war we'd have overlapping tours that allowed us to get to know each other well, trading shooting techniques as well as stories. Three years after attending Camp Perry as a civilian, I participated in shooting competitions as a member of the Marine Corps, representing my attack squadron and winning the Individual Service Rifle Award in 1965. I wasn't a bad shot from the seat of a jet either, I might add.

In Vietnam, when I'd begun working with Viet Cong guerrillas and North Vietnamese Army regulars who saw the wisdom of defecting to our side, raids with my new soldiers yielded a lot of weapons—most collected off their dead former compatriots. The real state of our enemy was evident in their weapons—a ragtag assembly of Chinese, Russian, French, and even American-made guns, the latter mostly dating back to the Korean and World War II eras. We even came across old US carbines to which I put my gunsmithing skills to work. I rebored the rifles and gave them to the scouts I was training, because, since most of them were small-bodied to start with and had suffered malnutrition while fighting for the Viet Cong, they couldn't travel far with the weight of an M14.

My own weapon of choice for search and destroy missions against the Viet Cong was a Thompson submachine gun. I liked the power and the rate of fire it produced. A person could lay out a pretty clear calling card with it. I didn't mind that there was something about the look of the gun that had a "don't fuck with me" quality to it either. I always figured it would be the gun John Wayne would carry if given a choice.

Much of my role as the head of the Kit Carson Scout Program was to intimidate the enemy enough to make it clear that a better choice for the Viet Cong would be to join us instead of fight us. I had to leave no doubt that the other option was a rather unpleasant death at the hands of my fellow Marines, who already had a fearful reputation among the Viet Cong. I had a reputation of my own, which came with a downside. When you had a high kill count, particularly one that most often came during sniping missions or special operations, you got a bounty put on your head. (I don't recall what the going rate was for a verified kill on Steve Luckey, but I'm guessing I'd be disappointed at the asking price.) I suppose it didn't help that when my boys killed a known Viet Cong target, we made sure to leave a calling card so the enemy would know who'd done the killing.

As a result of the bounty on my head, I ate, slept, and shat with my .45 and I spent more than my share of time with the M1 and the M14 as well. You'd think some people would get tired of guns if they had to eat and sleep with them all the time, but to me it was like having a reliable tool, and a mechanic never gets tired of a good wrench. My sniping weapon of choice was a Remington 700 BDL. It was a simple weapon, one that held up well in the awful wet, humid conditions of the jungle. Easy to work on and maintain, I shot regularly at 1,000 yards, and it was accurate out to 2,000 yards.

Upon my return from Vietnam, most of my shooting was confined to a more normalized kind of hunting for game meat. I left the Marines and joined the ranks of pilots at Northwest Orient Airlines, although I continued to train and consult with South Korean and other military units (as well as US law enforcement and intelligence agencies) on tactics of the innovative work I was involved with in Vietnam as well as in weapons training. While still in the Marine Corps I was a part-time deputy sheriff in Florida and Alabama, and while flying for Northwest I was a reserve deputy for the Ramsey County Sheriff's Office in St. Paul, Minnesota. Once again, carrying a gun became an official act for me. Law enforcement work augmented the pay of this new pilot on the bottom of the union totem pole, and it helped carry me through strikes and layoffs—which weren't uncommon in what was a turbulent time for the industry.

At the beginning of 1974, my personal relationship with guns changed in an unexpected way when Donald W. Nyrop, CEO of Northwest Airlines, issued a letter officially authorizing me to carry a sidearm "on or about my person" as an officer on the flight deck and when deadheading as a crew member on any Northwest flight.

Nyrop's desire to arm me had been a little over two years in the making. It was part of his reaction to an infamous event in American aviation history—the D.B. Cooper hijacking of a Northwest 727 between Portland and Seattle on November 24, 1971. (Dan Cooper was the pseudonym under which the hijacker bought his ticket, but D.B. made it into public record after a reporter created a typo in his coverage of the event). At any rate, he made off with a $200,000 ransom—equivalent of about $1.2 million today—by parachuting from the rear steps of the airplane into remote terrain near the Lewis River in Washington. While a small amount of the money was found by a boy a decade later near the Columbia River in 1980, neither Cooper nor his parachute was ever located. Personally, I doubt that he survived the jump, but the bad taste of losing two hundred grand never left Nyrop.

Nyrop declared that he would never pay another "goddamn ransom" again. He began talking with those in federal law enforcement and federal aviation circles (he'd once run the Civil Aeronautics Board, predecessor to the Federal Aviation Administration), pondering ways to put a stop to hijackings. Ideas included training FBI agents to fly commercial airliners.

I didn't know any of this. At the time of the D.B. Cooper hijacking, I'd been in Seattle to celebrate Thanksgiving with my cousin Edie. Our Thanksgiving-eve dinner was interrupted by a phone call summoning me to the airport. Alongside law enforcement personnel and other Northwest employees, I watched as the hijacked plane refueled. Amid discussions of the hijacker's unusual request for two parachutes, there was talk of sending a Northwest chase plane with me at the controls. I remember one FBI lead agent preaching about the finesse required in such situations, while another agent whispered that he wanted nothing more than authorization to storm the plane and kill Cooper. The dichotomy of those two positions was the epitome of a larger divide throughout both law enforcement and the airline industry regarding counter-hijack response. Questions only intensified among pilot ranks over the next weeks when it appeared that Cooper had disappeared off the face of the planet. Hijacking had accelerated, encouraged not just by his disappearance but by the realization that taking a plane could be a lucrative means of extortion. Added to this, of course, was the bonus of an ultimate media stage.

For those of us flying the planes, a lot of mental energy went toward preparing for the next hijacking as well as worrying about hijack methods that were growing more extreme and more bizarre. 1972 would become the worst year on record for hijackings. By then, colleagues on flight decks across the country were being taken as hostages every week. From the view of the cockpit, it felt like there was a hijacking every day. In later years, hijacks evolved into strange and unpredictable responses to the Mariel boatlift of 1980 and its mass emigration of Cubans to Florida. Some hijackers sided with the Cuban exiles, more with Castro and the revolution, but nearly all seemed to want to fly to Cuba to get their names in the papers and make some grand political statement. Those of us responsible for the safety of our crews and passengers were no more than pawns in this game played out by men who were often quite disturbed and always delusional.

Our bosses were sending us one message—comply with demands no matter how ridiculous to ensure that no one gets hurt, while the FBI and others were sending another—teach hijackers a lesson that will register with any copycats. We had little choice but to await the day that our number was called and an armed hijacker would knock on the cockpit door, holding a gun to a flight attendant's head. And we had little choice but to laugh alongside the rest of the country as Saturday Night Live spoofed the hijackers' "take me to Cuba" line, even if our laughter was uncomfortable to say the least.

Focused on keeping my charges safe and getting enough flying time to pay bills in an era of strikes and work stoppages, I was taken by surprise the day I was summoned to Nyrop's office. What would the CEO want with me? Curious, I had no idea what to expect. Nyrop asked me a little bit about my background and about my service in Vietnam and told me that the next time someone tried to hijack a Northwest plane, he wanted to kill the son of a bitch.

"We're done giving money to hijackers. The next time some asshole thinks he can take control of a Northwest plane, I want to put a stop to it by whatever means necessary," he said. "Captain Luckey, I've been informed that you're the man I need. From everything I've been told, I know you can get this job done."

I responded, "Sir, I don't know that I can do that."

Nyrop, his eyes appearing larger because of the thick, horned-rimmed glasses he wore, said, "I know you can do it."

I clarified my hesitation. "No, I know I can take care of the problem. I just don't know if I can do that legally."

"You let me take care of what's legal," he replied.

I have no idea what all was involved in behind-the-scenes deals brokered by Nyrop in Washington, DC, but he clearly used his clout. I've been told by others that when he approached the FBI about arming pilots and needing FBI expertise to do it, he was told, "But Mr. Nyrop, you already have the perfect man flying for your operation."

What I do know is that in January of 1974 I was summoned back to corporate headquarters and told that a letter from Mr. Nyrop, authorizing me to carry a weapon on board, would be waiting for me. The airlines and the FBI needed someone who was equally adept at flying a commercial airliner and remaining steady under fire. They needed a shooter who could fly.

I was supposed to pick up the letter from Captain Hockburn, the general manager of flight operations for Northwest. Hockburn was an intimidating guy. He'd been around Northwest forever, was frustrated with overseeing flight operations in such an unpredictable time, and definitely thought Northwest's old guard had earned the right to direct policy. I was a young pilot with a reputation and confidence that a guy like Hockburn probably found cocky.

When I arrived at Hockburn's office, I said, "Sir, I'm here to pick up a letter that Mr. Nyrop has left for me."

Hockburn opened the right-hand drawer of his desk, retrieved a page typed on Northwest letterhead, and slid it across the desk.

"Yeah, I know about your letter," he said. He looked at me with a mixture of fear and scorn. I didn't understand what had made him react as he had. I thanked him, took the letter and turned to leave his office.

Hockburn stopped me. "Luckey, I'm going to tell you something. You scare the shit out of me. They ought to keep you in a cage and only let you out when they need you." Apparently, my reputation from Vietnam had preceded me to his office.

Soon after retrieving my letter from Mr. Nyrop, I was told to report to a shooting range outside Minneapolis for training with the FBI. I joined eight other Northwest pilots who'd all been carefully selected and who all came from military backgrounds. Leading our training was Special Agent Bob Taubert, an expert on small arms and close-combat assault. We set up chairs in the layout of a cockpit and began simulated training for an armed assault coming through the cockpit door. Any shooting we might have to do in a hijacking would inevitably involve an intruder holding a flight attendant or passenger hostage, probably at direct gunpoint. This wasn't a situation encountered on any shooting range or even in military combat. There was no room for error. And any encounter would happen at close range.

An aircraft is a unique environment. It's not exactly as if you can open a door and walk out to safety. In terms of defense, you're up there entirely on your own. Of course, it also involves a vehicle with a cruising speed of 570 miles per hour that could, in the wrong circumstance or in the absence of a flight crew, crash and kill everyone on board. This was, by definition, specialized training.

The FBI had expertise in weapons training and hostage situations. What they didn't have was knowledge of a commercial aircraft or the nature of flight operations within a major airline. Working together in the training environment, we quickly learned that, at least in the case of a hijacker entering the flight deck, the ideal counter-assault would come from a right-handed shooter in the copilot's seat. Anything else needed to counter a hijacking attempt would be a fly-by-the-seat-of-the-pants operation, adjusting instantly to the shifting and unpredictable demands of a high-pressure situation—exactly my specialty.

Ultimately, armed with Mr. Nyrop's letter and the legal precedent of the 1958 Federal Aviation Act, I carried a weapon on all of my flights for nearly twenty years, until 1994 when the act was repealed and pilots were no longer authorized to carry firearms on board. Although I'd do it again in a heartbeat, taking on that kind of responsibility is demanding. I so believe in the deterrent power of arming willing pilots as a threat against potential bad guys that I spent considerable time fighting for that right, joining the Gore Commission and lobbying throughout Washington DC. I'll dig into that period of my life later, but my advocacy for the Federal Flight Deck Officer Program came from the old belief that "you've got to walk the walk to talk the talk."

Carrying a weapon in public is weighted with responsibility, although reminders of that responsibility don't always come in predictable ways. Once I had authorization from the FBI to carry a weapon when I flew, I chose a Smith & Wesson Model 19. I preferred the four-inch barrel because it came in and out of a holster nicely. The gun I carried was an FBI issue chambered for a .357 Magnum. I carried that weapon any time I was in the cockpit. The FBI had equipped me with special ammunition designed specifically for the environment of an airliner where there were almost always civilians present in a potential firing zone and there was an abundancy of sensitive electronic equipment that wouldn't do well if it were the victim of a bullet.

The .357 Magnum cartridges were clear, fashioned from a polymer that was extremely strong and could withstand the velocity of exiting a gun barrel while maintaining precise trajectory. I loved the Model 19 because it was so reliable, and the .357 offered good firepower. The FBI engineers had done a good job developing a cartridge that maintained the weapon's reliability. Inside the cartridge were three small pellets. The cartridge was designed so that it would enter a target and then break apart, sending the pellets laterally. The design was intended that the bullet would enter a body, do maximum damage, but not leave the intended target. Anyone who's spent much time firing weapons knows that the made-for-TV depictions of hiding behind a wall or a car door doesn't actually provide much protection from a traditional shell. But in this case, the bullets were designed for a very specific purpose—making a kill in a hostage situation. The pellets' lateral movement meant that any well-placed center shot would inflict severe damage on one or more vital organs. It was ammunition built for close range in a place where you were trying to protect others. To use it, you'd be looking your victim in the eye.

It was my habit during my flying days that as soon as I reached my lodging for the night's layover, I'd go to my room, remove my weapon from my holster, and empty it of ammo. I'd place the ammunition in an ashtray, return the gun to my holster, and then go take a shower. I've spent my life around guns and know how to use them, but to enter an evening on a layover with friends knowing I didn't have the responsibility of being armed was always a pleasure. As I said, there's a responsibility that comes with carrying a weapon in public, and it's one that I didn't take lightly. Once I was done flying for the night, I wanted to relax, have a few drinks with friends, and drop the hyper-vigilance I carried with me on the job.

One night on a layover in Cleveland at the Holiday Inn where always stayed, I exited the shower, still just wrapped in a towel, to find my friend and fellow pilot, Bill Felinger, in my room. I always enjoyed flying with Bill. He was a bit of a screwball who was up for most anything and an all-around good guy. We shared a lot of the same interests, including pleasure taken in shooting. Because he knew of my expertise with weapons, he'd bought a .357 model that was identical to mine. I'd even helped him sight it in when visiting him at his home.

Despite knowing Bill well, I was still taken by surprise to find him attempting to perform a quickdraw with my gun in front a mirror. Poorly, I might add, catching the weapon on the holster and nearly fumbling it. "What in the hell are you doing," I shouted. "That's no toy."

His reply to being caught was, "This holster is a piece of shit."

"Nah," I told him. "You're doing it wrong." The holster was specifically designed to be concealed under a suit jacket or light coat, and one I had chosen with the same care with which I chose the weapon it holstered.

"What do you mean?" he asked.

"Let me show you," I said. I took the gun and the holster from him, put it on, and then, facing the same mirror, performed a quickdraw much like I'd done during shows back at McTool's gun club. I performed the move flawlessly, as I had a thousand times before but found myself momentarily speechless when, at the end of the maneuver, the damned thing went off. The son-of-a-bitch had put ammo in it. I smelled the cordite of a live shell leaving a barrel and heard the ring of a gunshot penetrating the exterior cinderblock wall of my hotel room. "What the hell did you do?" I demanded.

"Me? You're the one that pulled the trigger."

"You loaded the damn thing."

"The weight wouldn't have been right otherwise."

"This is bad," I said. "Everybody had to have heard that. If the FBI finds out, I'm sunk."

"Forget the FBI," Bill said. "If the airline finds out, we're done."

"Shit," I said. "This is bad. Really bad," I said, as I looked at the ragged hole the bullet had left in the wall. I emptied the weapon and holstered it, looking incredulously at Bill. I pictured the arrival of

police while I was dressed in nothing more than a towel and trying to
explain that I was licensed to carry the gun. "What are you even doing
here?" I asked Bill.

"I was down in the bar. You were supposed to be down there
a half hour ago."

I shook my head in disbelief as I scrambled to get dressed.
Gradually it occurred to me that there had been no commotion, no
noises in the hall, no sirens, no knocks at the door. I gave it another
minute. Then I looked at Bill. Was it possible that no one had noticed?
I looked around the room, then began picking up little pieces of
cinderblock that littered the carpet below the hole. These I tossed in
the toilet and flushed it. "This is what's going to happen," I told Bill.
"I'm going to go to the hardware store and get something to patch this
hole. You're going to go down a floor, find a room that's open and cut
out a piece of wallpaper so we can cover this up. Someplace
inconspicuous."

"How am I supposed to do that?"

"Get creative," I told him.

The hallways were quiet. I went down a set of back stairs and
didn't encounter anyone. Maid carts sat idle before closed doors. When
I got back from the hardware store, all remained as if nothing had
happened. Bill was there, smiling and proudly showing me a scrap of
wallpaper. "I moved a bed," he said, "and cut it out where nobody can
see it. All the maids must be on break or something. A bunch of the
rooms were open." I shrugged, still wondering if we had a chance to
get away with this. I'd bought a putty knife and some plaster and got
to work.

By the time we were done, we were pretty proud of our work
and anxious to get out of the hotel and get a drink. The next morning,
when we met the rest of our crew to take the shuttle to the airport, Bill
and I looked at each other, raised our eyebrows and winked. We
couldn't believe we'd gotten away with it.

Two years later, Bill and I both found ourselves on Cleveland layovers and staying at our regular old haunt. After dinner Bill and I had stayed on at the bar to catch up. He had made captain, and we missed flying together. The hotel manager, a guy that we'd known for years, stopped by and asked if he could join us. He liked to flirt with our flight attendants and always seemed interested in our flying adventures. We swapped a few stories. A couple of drinks later, he put down his drink, looked me in the eye, and with a smirk, asked me, "So, for the longest time, I've been wanting to ask what in the hell were you two shooting at when you took out a chunk of my wall?"

I nearly spit out my drink. "You knew about that?"

"Knew about it? The entire hotel heard the shot. I asked my security guy to go check it out, and he told me I didn't pay him enough." The hotel manager started laughing as he told his story. "I knew I had Steve Luckey staying with us that night and figured it pretty much had to be you two. Man, you had things stirred up. I had maids hiding in closets. Two of them said they were hiding under a bed and somebody came in and moved the bed with them under it, then moved it back again. A regular slapstick. The next morning, after you guys checked out, I went up to your room. You did a shitty job of patching up that hole. I had to bring a guy in and do it right." He laughed harder still. "Just what were you two shooting at?"

Incidents with guns seldom offered such comedy. In truth, being armed in public changes your interactions with people, for you must always think about the safe-keeping of the weapon, the perception of others should they see it, and a tactical viewpoint of your surroundings. I was an expert at that already—Vietnam had taught me. And in those early days of commercial flying I already employed passenger screening and meaningful profiling, even though the airlines, including my employer, were slow as snails to do so. I'd watch passengers board my plane and I'd look for telltale signs of who might cause trouble, whether as a belligerent drunk or a would-be hijacker. Part of that vision is a shooter's vision.

Because I was good at what I did and because the FBI recognized my value, my role and my opportunities expanded. I moved on to complete full FBI SWAT training, which led to my utilization in a number of hijack situations. In nearly every hijacking the plane had to make an unscheduled landing, either because the hijacker wished to fly to a distant location or had specific ransom demands. At the very least the aircraft needed to take on fuel, but in cases where hijackers wished to abscond with the plane to an international destination, the plane needed a relief crew. Sometimes it was necessary to exchange one aircraft for another with a longer-range capability.

It was during these flight delays that the FBI sprang into action. Some of those actions were pretty extreme, such as the incident on July, 1971 when FBI sniper Kenneth Lovin killed hijacker Richard Obergfell. Obergfell had requested a new plane, and the FBI bought time by telling him they would have to shuttle him from LaGuardia Airport to a new plane waiting on the tarmac at Kennedy. Lovin took the shot as Obergfell disembarked the shuttle bus. Another incident occurred in Orlando, Florida in 1972 when the FBI attempted to immobilize a hijacked plane by shooting its tires out.

In 1983, I was present in Portland, Oregon when Glenn Tripp, a two-time hijacker, was shot and killed at close range by FBI agents. I'd been summoned in case the opportunity arose for me to slip on board. In an emergent procedure for managing active hijackings, the FBI constructed scenarios for a clean shot or a means to get agents in place who could surprise the hijacker. The FBI, in agreement with what Donald Nyrop had proposed, reasoned that if a certified pilot was on board—one who was also trained and capable of dispatching a hijacker if needed and if the situation allowed—then the tables might be turned.

Though we didn't know it at the time of the 1983 Portland incident, Tripp was already known to the FBI. Three years earlier, at the age of seventeen, Tripp hijacked a plane that was in route from Portland to Seattle. Sound familiar? It should. Tripp had chosen the same model of plane from the same airline—Northwest—flying the same route that D.B. Cooper had made infamous. Tripp carried a briefcase that he said contained a bomb. Eventually, during negotiations with the FBI, he made a demand for cheeseburgers and a rental car. When he deplaned in order to retrieve his demanded burgers, FBI agents took their advantage and shoved him into an awaiting car, arresting him without incident. At trial, Tripp was presented by his lawyers as developmentally disabled, possessing the mind of a ten or twelve-year old. He was ultimately sent to a home for disabled youth and placed on twenty years of probation.

Three years later, in a route reversal from Seattle to Portland, Tripp again hijacked a plane—this time carrying a shoebox that he claimed to contain a bomb. The FBI negotiated with Tripp for release of his hostages, gaining time by holding the plane for refueling which they'd told Tripp was necessary in order to reach San Diego. (Tripp had changed his plan, demanding now to be taken to Afghanistan.) Meanwhile, as I flew inbound to Portland, we discussed over a secure radio channel the likelihood of getting me on board posed as part of the maintenance crew.

I arrived at the remote runway where the hijacked plane was held only minutes after the FBI had brought the situation to an end. Negotiators succeeded in persuading Tripp to release half of the forty-one hostages. While those chosen for release evacuated the plane by an emergency slide, FBI agents, hoisted onto their colleagues' shoulders, breached the plane through a cockpit window. The first agent on board pushed through the narrow cockpit door and confronted Tripp in the first-class passenger cabin. Startled, Tripp moved to throw the shoebox at the agent, and the agent fired, killing the hijacker.

I boarded the plane shortly thereafter, saw Tripp's body, and noticed a young FBI agent seated in the first row. The agent was visibly shaken. Glancing from the body to the agent and surmising what had taken place, I turned to the young agent and said, "Well, he's a little small, but are you gonna mount him?"

The agent looked at me incredulously.

I said, "He's your first kill, isn't he? Aren't you going to mount him?"

A look of relief came over the agent's face and he laughed. I'd been in enough similar situations to know when you needed a little humor to diffuse things. Of course, if I'd arrived a few minutes earlier, it may well have been me in that agent's shoes. I'd been there before. And that young FBI agent had joined a very small society of brethren that every law enforcement officer hopes to avoid. I hope my gallows humor helped ease him through that moment, but I know firsthand that he would never be quite the same person again.

I was involved in that kind of work regularly for eleven years, ever since the day I was selected as one of twelve pilots to receive FBI specialized training as part of Operation Switch. In the years that followed, if I wasn't on the scene itself, I was called in as a consultant to the FBI for advice or information. Eventually the rank of pilots with specialized security training and knowledge grew to four, and we'd represent pilot organizations at the official request of federal aviation and law enforcement communities. At least one of us was called by the incident command center every time an event occurred.

Sometimes my involvement was far more ... shall we say ... direct, and it wasn't unusual to receive a call prompting me to hightail it to a location where an incident was unfolding. I recall one event during a hot summer in the 1980s that took place in a building rather than on a plane. Two escaped convicts had holed up in the US Treasury Building in DC. My mission was to be a pawn in their demand to be flown out of the city on a Northwest jet. Off I went. I was dispatched as their pilot and tour guide. I boarded the intended plane, and while performing pre-flight checks I hid several weapons in preparation for a worst-case scenario. I lucked out on that one, because the escaped prisoners surrendered after the FBI turned off all the air conditioning systems in the Treasury Building. The would-be hijackers gave up in the sweltering heat —just the kind of creative problem solving I like best.

To my mind, even more important than stopping a highjack in action was preventing one from happening in the first place. Hijackers needed to realize the dark fate that awaited them, and experience in the following years supported my belief. Although we continued to see occasional hijackings well into the mid-1980s, their frequency dwindled from one a week in 1972 to one a year in 1974. That happened to be the same year pilots began training with the FBI. I don't think that was a coincidence. That year we finally received other preventative tools as well when the Nixon Administration forced the hands of airline executives, mandating that every passenger would be screened and that all carry-on bags would be x-rayed.

I was a damn good pilot, but had I not earned the reputation as a good shooter, I'd have never been called into Nyrop's office and would never have worked with the FBI. No doubt I would never have become chairman of the security committee for the Air Line Pilots Association (ALPA), a role that allowed me to complete some of the most important work of my life. My experience as a shooter was largely responsible for the mindset and philosophy that I've built, and also for my reputation among friends and colleagues as the guy told to "make it happen, captain."

Participation in shooting, both as hunter and recreationist, has continued throughout my life. My side gig as a gunsmith in Minneapolis led to contacts which, in turn, presented opportunities in Montana leading big-game hunting parties. Eventually those excursions made me want to live in Montana full time. As a way to help justify the move, I founded 46 Outfitters and led elk and bear hunts in the Tobacco Root Mountains. That business grew after I retired from flying.

It was shooting that got me into security work in the first place, and working as a security consultant had taken me all over the world. While with ALPA I created the International Aviation Security Academy, serving as its lead instructor alongside a number of handpicked aviation security experts and writing most of its curriculum. The academy offered comprehensive security training and included a great deal of simulated shooting training.

I flunked out of retirement from Northwest at least three different times. While in post-retirement I formed a security consulting and training company named Jetana, and I also worked as an expert consultant for NEMO Arms. As a security consultant in 2003, I joined my long-time buddy Butch Luker playing in the sandbox of Saudi Arabia—he was a retired FBI agent with expert security knowledge of the aviation industry. There we led training for a 7,000-man defense force tasked with protecting the king's oilfields and Aramco's production facilities.

Until quite recently, as age and health have caught up with me (I guess that happens to the best of us, though I'd still be happy to go a few rounds if you ask me), I regularly returned to the patterns of my youth, continuing to hunt. My life in Montana feels like an echo of my childhood in the Poconos. The mountains are bigger, as is the game, but the rhythms of life are familiar. Blessed as we are, I bought a ranch in Pony, Montana, where the views are long and the wild comes right up to the back door. Wildlife on and near the ranch is abundant. I'm still pretty damn good at shooting a muskrat moving across the water or a gopher popping his head out of a hole. Turns out that woodchuck training has paid off after all.

I'm Fine and Don't Need a Thing

"Out here, due process is a bullet." —from
The Green Berets

My mother saved every letter I ever sent to her and my dad during my thirteen-month tour in Vietnam from 1966 to '67. She was that kind of mother. I guess the damn things are historical documents and belong in an archive now. I was a good son. I wrote often. When I read those letters now, I'm intrigued to see that, almost without fail, I signed them, "I'm fine and don't need a thing." Of course that was a lie. And also it wasn't.

I saw a lot I don't care to remember while in Vietnam, but I've never felt as alive or as useful. What I couldn't know then was that in those thirteen months I'd learn the lessons and the skills that I'd apply throughout the rest of my life. I also made many contacts that guided my future and certainly formed the core beliefs that have sustained me.

My time in Vietnam, as for all who served in that war I suppose, was complicated. There aren't a lot of men who I served with left to swap stories. Most of the men I worked closely alongside were either my superiors and decades older than me, or they didn't make it out. Or they were Vietnamese, as you'll learn more about. Any reunion I would attend could be held in a phone booth.

It's true that Vietnam was miserable. It wasn't unusual for the temperature to reach well into the triple digits and it could stay nearly that hot even when it rained, which it often did for weeks on end. There was a wet season and a dry season and the wet season seemed to last forever. During the wet season, it might drizzle one minute and come down in buckets the next. Sometimes it seemed like it did both. Trench foot and jungle rot was as expected as a whore with VD. You couldn't get away from the heat. When I was operating off of Hill 55, I'd go on a four-mile perimeter hike and would have to wring my clothes out when I got back. If you had to climb a hill with full gear, your lungs would burn and it felt like what I experienced working fire lines back in the Pennsylvania woods, my lungs wanting to crumple and turn to ash. The Vietnam I experienced was filled with hills and cliffs and green mountains. The jungle was thick and the bamboo grew so close together that you would need a chainsaw to cut a hundred yards in an hour. When climbing the side of a mountain in a rain forest, foot-long leaches would drop on you, and peeling them from your skin was like tearing an adhesive bandage off in one painful rip.

As awful and as lethal as the jungle was, it was beautiful. I saw elephants and tigers and every variety of snake. There was even a nine-foot-long species of ocean-going snake that had lethal venom for which there was no antidote. I imagine that if it didn't scare you to death, the hours between a bite and meeting your maker would prove interesting ones. There were monkeys everywhere. They were cute but unnerving because they tended to hide in the bushes and trees alongside trails and then take off screaming, a sure bet for getting a skittish Marine to let loose with bursts of automatic weapon fire while screaming, "Ambush!" Then, of course, the risk of ambush became real since the monkeys had exposed your position.

Some guys came down with everything: malaria, dysentery, Hepatitis C, various STDs, and lots and lots of FUOs (fevers of unknown origin). We ran into booby traps that shot spikes into you that the VC covered with shit so that pathogens would get into your bloodstream. We drank from streams and crawled in mud filled with crap and blood and who knows what else. I guess I've got an iron stomach because I seldom had the runs and I ate a good deal of the local food—in villages, in Da Nang, and in the jungle. I thought there wasn't anything much better than finding fresh fruit (I practically existed on longan and wild bananas) while working my way through the jungle after a kill mission, with the exception of beer, which I was quite gifted at procuring. Sometimes it pays to be a bit of a comedian and to make friends easily.

I suffered through all the expected maladies of combat that everyone else did in that wet place—shin fungus and ringworm were common annoyances. If the food or the hills or the heat didn't get you, the bugs did. A state of being was to be hot, wet, filthy, and covered with bugs from asshole to appetite. The first months were pure misery. The misery continued but I learned not to give a damn about it. In the end, that's the recipe for how you survive a war. Frankly, you aren't left with much of any other choice.

Death was everywhere and it was nearly always unpredictable. When I wasn't facing the immediate presence of death in a low-flying airplane or in the midst of a firefight on the ground, it lurked in the shadows. The VC loved to attack in bad weather, moving in close with the cover of clouds and rain, exactly the opposite of what we had been trained to expect of a conventional enemy and seemingly intent on adding to our misery. Death could arrive on any night beyond the guarded wire of our headquarters in Da Nang, always within easy reach of a mortar shell. Death awaited you in booby traps, in tunnels that transected the jungle like a city sewer system where you might encounter half an army or one lone snake (the one as lethal as the other). You could find death in the scope of a competing sniper, in ambush patrols, in firefights that erupted out of thin air and that dissipated like so much smoke. Because cutting new trails through the jungle was so labor intensive it was impractical, we were stuck using existing ones and they were certain to be thick with well-disguised booby traps and mines. The Vietnamese may be the cleverest people in the world. The great majority of our causalities came at the hands of these hidden lethal contrivances.

I led small patrols in a manner mimicking the stealth of the VC, but we also traveled in huge convoys. We'd put four men with Thompsons in the back of every truck along with a swivel-mounted .50 caliber machine gun on the cab. The VC must have watched a few good American Westerns because they were experts at mounting ambushes at mountain passes where there was a bottleneck. Their opponent's lead vehicle would hit a landmine, stopping the entire convoy, and then their fun would begin. The VC would open up with .75-millimeter recoilless rifles. You had to be lucky not to get a hole or two in your hide while you scrambled to get under the truck. Nothing like a few .75 rounds to give a man some rapid religion. I served with some of the holiest bastards on the face of the earth, including a master sergeant who'd been in eleven such convoy ambushes just that year. He claimed to love every minute of it, but then he didn't have anything but white hair on his head and he was only thirty-eight years old.

I courted death regularly and brazenly by doing stupid but necessary shit like driving around known enemy locations in a Jeep, blaring propaganda from loudspeakers I'd rigged myself. I saw far too many young men die. I killed too many others to maintain an accurate count. And yet, I must still admit a sizable part of me loved my time in Vietnam.

That's a hard thing to explain to those who have never experienced combat. It's even a hard thing for many who have. I've been an adrenaline junkie all of my life—I always drove the fastest cars, flew the most powerful jets, hunted in the most challenging terrain for the biggest animals—and there is something addicting about the rawness of combat. I came to crave it. In combat, my senses were heightened, colors seemed more vivid, time slowed down. I got a kind of tunnel vision where some details attracted my closest attention and others dropped out entirely. Adrenaline flooded my body. The rest of the world fell away. I still miss the adventure and I still miss the brotherhood.

I had a beautiful wife and a young child waiting for me at home, and I desperately wanted to return to them. But I came extremely close to accepting the opportunity to re-up. Were it not for having a family, I likely would have accepted offers—they came regularly and were impassioned—to become part of a clandestine force not bound by the military code of conduct. To have the freedom and adventure of a kind of freelance warrior was more than tempting.

I had arrived as a pilot but my flying time was relatively short lived. Although I was assigned quite a number of missions flying the A-4, the simple truth was that there were more jet pilots than the war required. They needed chopper pilots, for helicopters were the workhorses of the war. I never liked the damn things. Too many fine pilots, dropping troops into hot landing zones with minimal resources to fight back, lost their live flying helicopters. It's not without irony that I grew so dependent on the damn things to extract me from clandestine missions. I had joined the Marines because I wanted to fly, but I counted myself lucky that I had other proven skills that made me valuable to senior officers on the ground—those smart enough to recognize that Vietnam was largely a war unlike the ones they'd been trained to fight. I was moved to ground operations.

As a result I was assigned to the commandant's office for most of my time in Vietnam, reporting directly to General Lewis W. Walt, commander of the III Amphibious Marine Force and the 3rd Marine Division. In the late spring and early summer, right after my reassignment, I actually straddled two fences, for I was appointed chief of psychological operations for all Marines in Vietnam while at the same time regularly flying missions with the 5th Air Commando Squadron. Believe me, I didn't get a lot of sleep. The one job would have been enough as I had 143 men reporting to me; I was in charge of all counter-intelligence operations; and I handled nearly all of the prisoners coming through the I Corps zone. The downside of my new responsibilities—I replaced a Lt. Colonel—was that I spent too much time stuck in an office. Any day that I spent at headquarters writing action reports, I'd long to be in combat. I wanted to be out in the woods. Returning from some fun in the jungle and being stuck on the desk was like going back to the schoolhouse after summer vacation.

The country was full of such contradictions. Competing enterprise, I guess you could say. At times, the people we were tasked with liberating from communism appeared hopeless in any sense of the word. To an American eye, theirs was the sort of life lived mostly by animals, and you could rarely place trust in any of them—which gave me my first exposure (of many to come) to a trust/verify environment. Sometimes that felt as true of the ARVN (the Army of the Republic of Vietnam), the South Vietnamese army that we were supposed to be supporting, as it did of the Viet Cong, guerrilla fighters intent on killing every last Marine. Vietnam seemed primitive. Grass huts in the villages, tin huts in the cities. No running water. Open fires for cooking. It felt like a place left behind by time.

Yet I was simultaneously aware that it was an ancient place, one where the way of life had hardly changed in centuries, families were close-knit, objects of prayer appeared in any given tree or rock altar. And here we were flying jets off aircraft carriers, dropping out of the sky from helicopters, eradicating the jungle with napalm, creating a wasteland with clusters of 500 and 750-pound bombs—unleashing all the components of modern warfare. The Vietnamese had a powerful advantage, though, for their culture believed that life after death would always be an improvement over their corporeal life. They were probably right because all of their time was spent at hard labor, fighting, or trying to scratch out survival. Few had any time for pleasure. They were long accustomed to others forcing foreign cultures on them, challenging their religion, their architecture, their food—the very foundations of their own culture. The French had set out to eradicate Buddhist culture and replace it with Catholicism. Why would the Vietnamese expect anything different from us?

I steadfastly believed in the rightness of our presence to root out communism. I worked tirelessly to educate the locals that Americans were not a carryover of the French colonialists. But they'd been told that we were cannibals, drinking the blood of their dead. I saw—even respected—both the resolve and the guile of our enemy who had ousted the Japanese and outlived the French. Most of them probably wanted no more than to go about their lives, tend their farms, and raise their families. I could see that even as I saw their bloodlust and their ruthlessness.

My fellow Marines could be just as confounding. I cherished the brotherhood I had joined and I was proud that we were a feared force, one eager to complete the jobs others could not. I liked that our enemy would behave differently if they knew American Marines were in the mix than they would if standing against ARVN or even the US Army. I would fight for every last Marine I served with. I had given an oath and I lived by it. Lew Walt could tell me to step in front of a bullet or to jump off a mountain, and I'd do it. I've been driven by patriotism my entire life and believed in a higher calling. Yet when troubles arose between civilians and Marines—the civilians were quick to throw bottles and rocks at convoys and to hang around the fenced perimeter of the base and taunt us—I saw fellow Marines shoot them off of bicycles, kick them off of motorcycles, and run them over with tanks. Because you couldn't discern who was a VC hiding among villagers or in the streets of Da Nang, we were left with little choice but to treat the whole country like a battlefield and the civilians like combatants.

The place seldom made any sense, and the only thing you could predict was to expect the unpredictable. In Vietnam I saw things that were morbid beyond the imagination of the most abstract mind. One day when I was out on patrol a M26 grenade landed thirty to forty yards from my position but didn't explode. I shot two bursts at it and hit it with eight out of fifteen rounds, but the thing still didn't explode even though it broke apart and the frag coil popped out. The very next night I was visiting one of my scouts who was laid up in the hospital with a combination of pneumonia and tuberculosis when they brought in a seaman off an English merchant ship. The sailor was dead as a doornail without a mark on him. Turns out he fell off a stool while tightening a bolt. Men were as likely to die in the arms of a whore as they were to be blown away at the wrong end of a gun or to wreck a Jeep while drunk or be taken out of combat by a mosquito.

Everyone who arrived in-country went through a learning curve. I expected the reality of combat to be different from training—in my case, years of training—but nothing could prepare me for it, and the very nature of the enemy's approach to combat wasn't something trainers had adapted to effectively. It took time not only to adjust to the heat and the weather but the culture as well. Actually, that's a lie; there was no way any of us could ever get used to the heat.

Days of boredom passed with the speed of slugs taking a nap and then the whole place erupted, sometimes only for a minute. If you spotted a VC moving at a distance, you might mistake him for a farmer or an old lady, and then he'd disappear before you could scratch your ass or raise your weapon. You were ten times more likely to happen upon the enemy where you didn't expect them than to fight them off the perimeter of a firebase or in an organized action. Most of the time you didn't have concrete evidence that they were anywhere near until the bullets started flying. But with time, I started to get a feeling for the enemy and the country. I equate most combat in Vietnam to deer hunting or fishing a good trout stream; unless you'd done it a few times and had a good teacher, you weren't going to get much in the way of results. I had plenty of good teachers and I was placed in the thick of action nearly immediately upon my arrival, so I got the experience I needed right away. I'm one of the lucky bastards who didn't get tagged while he was still green.

Vietnam, a place as seemingly opposite of Pennsylvania as any I can imagine, fit me somehow. Whereas most men would come back from search and destroy missions several pounds lighter, I tended to put on weight. When my tour was completed and I returned stateside, a nurse double-checked the scale during my physical and said, "This can't be right."

Once I was assigned to General Walt's command staff, I felt I was among kindred spirits. I was the only lieutenant on a staff that was nearly all colonels and above. General Walt and I had a lot in common. He was a competitive shooter and a guy with a Special Forces background. Walt saw things differently than most high-ranking officers and was ahead of his time when it came to understanding how to combat an elusive enemy like the Vietnamese. Vietnam was the third war he had served in and he'd won two Navy Crosses for extraordinary heroism during World War II. *Life* magazine wrote a cover story about him in May of 1967, shortly after I'd returned stateside. Much of the article focused on his development of an innovative program called the Combined Action Program. The program evolved from a larger philosophy that Walt had developed. It consisted of squads of Marine and Navy medical corpsmen who volunteered for combined action platoons that partnered with forces from the ARVN. These combined platoons operated mainly in villages and hamlets and were focused on denying the Viet Cong access to the people living there. Their orders were to help protect the villages, get to know the people, find the local Communist infrastructure and root it out.

Walt understood that if we had any chance of winning the war, we had to win the confidence of ordinary Vietnamese citizens. Walt was ahead of his time, and it's thinking like his that has become more common now in insurgent wars, although it seems to me that we largely have to keep relearning his lessons again and again. He was a good Marine. He answered to the chain of command, but he thought in different patterns; and there was a lot of action he led that wasn't the kind of things written about in *Life* magazine.

General Walt and I had a unique and special relationship. He treated me like a son. He recognized my abilities as a shooter, knew I was a good Marine, and respected my intelligence. I suspect it was his recognition of the value of someone who could shoot that got me stationed under his command in the first place. I remember him saying once, "I have a lot of tough Marines and I have a lot of smart Marines, but I don't have many tough, smart Marines." Through General Walt, I began to spend a lot of time working with Special Forces units, particularly those of the 9th Marines stationed out on Hill 55 as well as with the 5th Special Forces Group. The 9th Marines, Alpha Company, 1st Battalion had been my first ground-duty station.

Hill 55 and Hill 5 were the only high points in the middle of a wide valley sixteen kilometers southwest of Da Nang, and the two hills stuck out like warts on a dog dick. Captain Edward Land had established a scout/sniper school there, and the hills offered no shortage of opportunities to practice sniping. Nearly every day in the hours just before dawn and dusk, we'd go hunting. From those fire posts, Special Forces units coordinated many of their incursions. I don't know how many times I rode out between Da Nang and those two hills, but we seldom made the trip without taking fire.

My duties under General Walt were varied, as were the operations his headquarters command oversaw; these included, among many other things, providing air support radar teams for ground combat troops. I was formally assigned to the 244th Psychological Operations Company, and many of my duties were linked to goals of the combined actions units—get to know the population, find the local Communist infrastructure, and then root it out. One aspect of our work was to distribute messages through broadcasts and leaflets. These were reminders to the Viet Cong that they were facing an elite fighting force that was not only infinitely better equipped with more ways of killing them, but which also offered them a safe-conduct pass should they surrender to any allied force. That's the work that had me ranging about on dangerous roads in a Jeep equipped with a loudspeaker system getting the hell shot out of me. There were a number of such ragtag "technologies" utilized in spreading our messages, but I found the most effective means of distribution for our flyers was to pin them to the dead bodies of Viet Cong. That didn't leave any room to read between the lines.

Rather than just bitch about the fighting conditions we faced and the tactics our enemy used against us, I quickly came to understand that you couldn't fight an unconventional enemy with conventional means. The reality of Vietnam was that most of the time you couldn't even identify your enemy, let alone defeat them using the tactics of past wars. To be successful in Vietnam, we didn't need to be armed with superior firepower as much as we needed superior intelligence. We needed to know our enemy if we were to understand their strategies.

Early on in my time in Vietnam, in May of 1966, a group of Viet Cong fighters surrendered themselves to Marines near Da Nang through the framework of an existing program known as Chieu Hoi. Also known as the Open Arms Program, Chieu Hoi literally translates from Vietnamese as "welcome return". It created mechanisms for deserters—Hôi Chánh—from the North Vietnamese Army (NVA) and Viet Cong to return to the South Vietnamese government. (The NVA was a guerrilla force that formally referred to itself as the Liberation Army of South Vietnam.) When a soldier deserted under this program, he was interviewed to determine his sincerity, rewarded for any weapons or equipment turned in, and placed in a reeducation program where he learned the aims and purposes of the government of South Vietnam and the role of the Free World Military Assistance Forces in the war. Many went on to serve with the ARVN.

In the case of the group that surrendered to our units, rumors began to spread among the local population that one of the deserters, Nu Van Bay, had been tortured and murdered by American soldiers. To defuse this rumor and expand the effectiveness of our psychological warfare operations, we had Nu Van Bay, along with two of his fellow Hôi Chánh, tour the nearby villages to personally refute the rumors and inform the people about the good treatment they'd received from the Marines. Almost immediately we saw a subsequent rise in the number of new Viet Cong deserters in the area. Seeing the success of such a psychological operation, I set out to expand a targeted version of the program and use it to build our counterinsurgency and intelligence.

Watching the reaction of local villagers to Nu Van Bay, I realized the power of the messages we could send. If leaflets dropped from the bullshit bomber along with announcements broadcast from the back of Jeeps offered calling cards to would-be deserters, seeing the efficient brutality waged by former comrades either enflamed them with new resilience or scared the living shit out of them to where working for our side could look pretty good. Those summer months offered me a great chance to screen several Hôi Chánh, focus on the reeducation of those I found to be sincere in their desire to turn against their former comrades, and utilize them as an intelligence source to demonstrate to my commanders and other Marine units how we might profit from their local knowledge. These were the infant months of what became the Kit Carson Scout Program.

I named the program in honor of the frontier hero Kit Carson, someone whose deeds of valor and bravery I'd grown up reading about. Carson—a trapper, scout, and guide—had worked safely in Indian country throughout the Rocky Mountain West in the 1840s. He crossed what is now Wyoming dozens of times, and he served as guide on several of the Fremont expeditions in the Northern Rockies, mapping what had only been fur-trading routes prior to then. Carson was universally described by those who knew him as cautious, modest, competent and cool-headed, always brave but never foolhardy. Fremont, who was brash and flamboyant, wrote vivid accounts of the expeditions and rose to great fame. Because of that, Carson also became quite well known—later becoming the subject of dime store novels that raised him to a kind of mythological status.

To me, Carson not only personified the American patriotic values of those ready to endanger their lives for the good of their nation, but he was relatable as an expert at hunting, trading, and scouting. More relevant to my program, he was adept at knowing how to understand and work with the enemy he fought. Kit Carson was known in equal measure for his ability to negotiate and trade with the enemy as well as understand their war tactics, beliefs, and ability to live off the land. First, I had to understand my enemy. Second, if we were really to get these guerrilla fighters to become assets in battling their former comrades, I had to find ways to convince them to adopt American values and standards. They had to come to believe in freedom and to trust not just American soldiers but the democracy they represented. If I could teach these Scouts that we weren't there to occupy their country permanently, I knew I could use their intimate knowledge of the Viet Cong and its terrain to assist us. Who, if not the former Viet Cong, would know where they stored supplies? Who better to show us the locations of tunnels, landmines, hidden explosives, and booby traps? It seemed perfectly logical to me that if you need to wipe your ass, you find the guy who makes the toilet paper.

Having experienced firsthand the cleverness, bravery, and tenacity that the Viet Cong routinely displayed, I'd come to respect them as warriors. At the core of my respect was a belief I've held onto in every element of my career in security and counterterrorism: You can't defeat a bad guy unless you learned to think like a bad guy. Maybe some of the lessons of my wayward youth paid off after all.

Of course, this was tricky business on many levels. Most of the Hôi Chánh were just sick of fighting, sick of suffering, and they were looking for a way to leave the war. Many were searching for what seemed a dignified means to surrender but they had no interest in fighting alongside allied forces. A tiny handful had actually become dismayed by Communist propaganda or felt abandoned by North Vietnamese leaders, recognizing they were being used as bodies in a war of attrition. On the other hand, a few radicals saw the opportunity to become double agents and use information they learned about us to gain access for deadly attacks. A big part of my job was to tell the difference among these motives. Doing so involved a whole lot of picking the fly shit out of the pepper.

A particularly effective deterrent for any deserters who proved less than sincere in their commitment to help us was to use their dead bodies as correspondence. If I took a traitor back to his home village, made a public display of his admission to being a double agent, then removed him from the gene pool in front of a lot of witnesses, other Viet Cong thought twice about following his lead.

The exceptional few who did prove loyal to us needed to become trusted members of our units. Most were lethal fighters and showed tremendous courage. Once they satisfied our judgment that they were sincere in defecting and were committed to fighting alongside us, it became essential that I found ways to make them feel like they belonged. We set about teaching them core American values and training them in US military approaches to chain of command and communication. Throughout its history, the greatest contribution to American military success is its emphasis on cementing absolute loyalty between one soldier and another. The interdependence and brotherhood that marks a Marine's commitment to his fellow Marine is the backbone of the Corps. We had to teach those values to the Scouts. The Viet Cong already understood loyalty to a cause, to their families, and to their home regions. Our job was to help them see that an American mission to halt communism was in line with the ideals of poor farmers trying to protect their homes and families at all costs. Essentially, we had to offer counterpropaganda to overcome the brainwashing that they'd suffered in their former Communist units. Most were poor, uneducated farmers simply intent on protecting their communal fields as they'd been forced to do all their lives against a string of enemies. Those my age and younger had been born into Japanese occupation. It was easy for the Communists to convince them that Americans were no different from the French and Japanese before them, invaders intent on staying and intent on ruling their lives.

In order to convince deserters to accept a different motivation for American involvement, Marines needed to accept the Scouts and treat them with respect. That meant learning enough about them and their culture so they would see us as worthy of their trust. But a reciprocal approach was also necessary, and, since they'd once been deadly enemies, this was no small undertaking.

A first step in my own relationship with the Scouts was to show them I could relate to them on a human level. The Scouts were all volunteers. And they came only from the ranks of guerrilla fighters in the Viet Cong—not the NVA. Upon entering our program, Scouts were provided comprehensive medical examinations and were given American uniforms, housing, food—all of the necessities expected by an American soldier that were non-existent or in short supply within the Viet Cong. We paid them a base salary higher than that of soldiers of the ARVN. We wanted to make sure the Scouts were viewed, in every way, as American soldiers.

As part of their training, Scouts were enrolled in rudimentary English classes. They needed to know enough essential English words and phrases to communicate simple information in the heat of combat. Meanwhile I learned a bit of Vietnamese, for attempting to learn their language showed respect.

I often bunked with them and I ate with them. If their families were in the immediate area of South Vietnamese control, I shared meals with the men and their families. Interacting with the Scouts was a mix of truly getting to know them as individuals while closely observing them to ensure the sincerity of their loyalty. Trust and verify. Once they'd proven themselves, I demonstrated that I would never ask something of them that I didn't ask of myself. Because I would fight for them and kill for them, they in turn did the same for me. As they displayed their value—which nearly always meant saving American lives during combat or by removing threats—they enjoyed growing respect from Marines.

Over time I became good friends with several Scouts—one in particular. Vo Cong and I became quite close. There is no doubt that he saved my ass on more than one occasion. Vo Cong had an uncle who owned a plantation near Da Nang and we were often invited to his home to dine. His uncle knew nearly all the VC in the area and so was an important source of information.

Eating at the plantation was an adventure in itself. Chow usually consisted of pho—Vietnamese traditional stew or broth served over thick noodles. There was always rice. I remember one of my first dinners there as clearly as if I ate it last night—we were served a soup that consisted of monkey, rice noodles, peppers, peanuts, bean sprouts, shredded coconuts, and bamboo shoots, all in a fishy broth. If you've ever been to an authentic Vietnamese restaurant or spent time in a predominantly Vietnamese neighborhood, then you've already experienced the acrid, pungent smell of fish base—a fermented oil from rotten fish mixed with garlic, a smell that permeates everything. I quickly learned to eat without inhaling. The Vietnamese love the stuff, but I found it nauseating. Every meal was washed down with a murky locally brewed beer-like drink called bah moi bah. Dessert consisted of a cane-and-seed baked candy and was completed by drinking Benedictine liqueur, a tradition inherited from the French.

Even though I never came to love fish broth, I enjoyed meals like this one greatly. I was a frequent dinner companion of the Vietnamese, dining with numerous contacts and friends which usually originated with my Scouts. Their hospitality in sharing such meals was always great, even if conditions were sometimes a bit on the unsanitary side. I believe that a lot of diplomacy was accomplished—and a great deal of intelligence gathered—by my willingness to eat everything my hosts did in exactly the manner they did, even if that included raw or even rotten fish. I learned the most amazing things at those dinners, and nearly everything I learned seemed to pan out as true.

Our Kit Carson Scouts proved themselves to be indispensable, particularly in safely directing search and destroy missions. By August of 1966 we had placed six Scouts within Marine platoons. The work the Scouts did was extraordinarily dangerous but effective. I had personally trained all six. In those early days, the only assistance I had was an experienced staff sergeant named George Handzo, a Pennsylvania coal cracker from Wilkes-Barre. George was a dozen years older than me and was a Korean War veteran, pushing twenty years in the Corps. We were eventually joined in our work of selecting, training, testing, and leading the Scouts by another staff sergeant, Teruo Taketomo.

By August, the program, though small, had shown such success that General Walt assigned Colonel Robert Read as the psychological operations officer to oversee the program with an eye toward expanding it exponentially. It grew slowly but steadily over the remainder of my time in Vietnam. I was detailed to chronicle our training procedures and selection processes, which allowed the program to expand to new units. By the end of 1971, there were over 2,000 Kit Carson Scouts.

Largely because of my work with the Scouts, I'd become a highly recognizable figure that drew the attention of my superiors. One day in August, I was pleasantly surprised to learn from General Walt that I was being promoted to captain. I was even more surprised on the night that I was summoned to attend dinner at General Walt's house. He pinned my captain's bars on me in front of dinner party guests that included none other than John Wayne and Martha Wray. The two legendary stars even presented me with a gift—a Nikon camera.

These Hollywood icons were touring the country as part of a USO operation, entertaining troops, attending functions, and talking with wounded soldiers in hospitals. Martha Wray, in particular, really threw herself into the work, far more than simply showing up for a press event. She spent a great deal of time at hospitals talking with soldiers individually and at length, and she also helped the nursing staff where she was able. Both celebrities were interested in seeing the "real" war, not just places where their handlers would rather have them appear.

Nodding toward me, Walt told them, "If you want to see action, stick with this guy." I spent several interesting days in the company of The Duke, which was nothing short of an amazing experience; I'd been a fan of his for as long as I could remember. He may have been a movie star, but he was the real deal, authentic not just in his patriotism but in meeting the kids on the frontline and seeing the action.

Bringing famous stars into the country was a natural form of pro-American propaganda, particularly when they were as pretty as Martha Wray and Ann-Margaret, who I also met. Nothing like palling around with movie stars to make your friends jealous. Of course, like other civilian enterprises, the USO made excellent cover for CIA operatives such as those responsible for Wayne and Wray.

While there was no doubt that General Walt was my champion, it was the work that we were accomplishing with the Kit Carson Scouts that gained me my promotion. My units proved extremely effective and they quickly developed a reputation. No operation that the Scouts performed was typical. We deployed a variety of approaches to win local populations and eradicate the VC. For example, during the July 1966 Operation County Fair alone, we identified and captured nineteen Viet Cong guerrillas due specifically to involvement by four of my initial Scouts.

A "county fair" was a large-scale operation using mixed-combat forces. We'd entirely surround a targeted village, then peacefully moved all the inhabitants to a temporary facility where we provided them medical care, warm meals, entertainment, and other services—with a little old-fashioned propaganda on the side. Through our broadcasts, villagers were told what was happening and that they'd be returned to their homes at the end of the day. They were required to bring identification credentials which would be scrutinized, and then new credentials were issued. The entire affair was a "hearts and minds" endeavor to remind villagers of the benefits of participating in a democratic society and of the type of care they could experience if they remained aligned with allied forces. They had the chance to see soldiers as humans. We talked with them, played games with the kids, and gave them treats. For most, the fair offered their first visit to a doctor or dentist. For many, the hot meals might've been be the first they'd had in some time.

While villagers were away from their homes attending the fair, Marines led by my Scouts swept their village, searching for VC tunnels, supplies, and operatives. It wasn't uncommon to find dozens of tunnels in a single village, often filled with Viet Cong weapons or supply caches. A Marine rearguard took up positions along likely escape routes to capture or engage any Viet Cong looking to flee. We hauled VC out of tunnels, destroyed supplies or returned them to civilian populations from where they'd been stolen, and shot down fighters scurrying like rats abandoning a sinking ship. In many instances, these county fairs gave Kit Carson Scouts an opportunity to identify Viet Cong officers who enjoyed protection from civilians, willing or not. Several were identified trying to blend in with fair attendees.

More often our operations were small in scale, with a Scout or two in a patrol-size unit on search and destroy missions to eradicate tunnels, clear booby-trapped trails, or cut off supply routes. Sometimes a mission focused on a targeted individual and might only include me with a Scout and a couple of Marines whose job it was to make sure I got my ass home. Sometimes I went on missions entirely alone, often acting upon information we might never have received if not for the Scouts.

The Kit Carson Scout Program had three essential goals: perform search and destroy missions (the heart of our work), gather intelligence, and win the psychological battlefront within villages. What we had stumbled ass-over-tea-kettle into was the battleground of insurgency. The work we'd accomplished in training for an insurgent war holds lessons for nearly all the recent theaters of war where American troops have fought; and they're elemental in combatting terrorism wherever it occurs.

The same can be said for second goal of the Kit Carson Scout Program—intelligence gathering—and it was always on my mind. I spent a great deal of time cultivating informants and those privy to the movements and actions of the Viet Cong. Much of what we did were real spook operations. Our directives and targets were often determined by intelligence gathered by CIA operatives, who were common in Da Nang particularly. Not only did these agents attach themselves to the USO, but they operated under the guise of US AID personnel and pretended to be employees of various government contractors and Western corporations that still had a presence in the country. We worked closely with Israelis and South Koreans, along with vestiges of the French intelligence units. A good number of critical missions assigned to me by General Walt were made possible by intelligence gathered by South Koreans, and I had the amazing experience of fighting alongside South Korean special forces units several times—among the bravest, most lethal forces in the world. Many intelligence relationships that I formed with other international operatives remained important contacts for decades after the Vietnam War, as the free world continued to encounter new enemies and new styles of warfare.

Among the information passed along by intelligence operatives or gathered during meetings with friendly contacts were identities of local VC commanders. Once we'd identified an obvious bad guy with enough authority to make other bad guys follow his orders, we presented our evidence to General Walt. And once General Walt was satisfied by the veracity of the intelligence provided, he'd greenlight a mission to remove the target.

General Walt was an officer of such high rank that he had Code Six clearance, which meant that he could move freely about the country and could commandeer any means of travel available be it a helicopter, a fixed wing aircraft, a patrol boat, or even a tank. He was privy to top secret information. He placed such trust in me and so believed in the critical nature of the missions he assigned me that he drafted orders extending his Code Six clearance to me.

Much to my surprise, I'd been assigned the role of paid assassin. It's an odd and unnerving position to find oneself in. It wasn't exactly the sort of the thing the world prepared me for, nor did Anna Cartwright. Actually, that's not true, for I think there were aspects of my childhood education—in Ms. Cartwright's classroom and in my father's hard teaching—that gave me the psychological profile for that type of work. I understood how to take highly unusual actions without surrendering my values or my mind in the process. My lasting comfort remains my confidence that I never killed anyone who wasn't deserving. In Vietnam, the Viet Cong leaders that we targeted were responsible for the deaths of hundreds, if not thousands—and among their victims were not just Americans or the South Vietnamese and other allied forces. The VC were also quick to starve their own people or kill them if they suspected them of aiding the South.

I was involved in such missions as often as twice a month. Sometimes they took place right at "home", in the heart of Da Nang. More often they were in combat zones, usually in small villages, although I also completed missions in Hue and in Huong Tra. More secretive still, and more controversial, were kill missions that took me into Laos and Cambodia—something that was officially forbidden. I was frequently supported by units that were part of the 5th Special Forces Group. Most insertions were via helicopter. Many were by parachute, most typically at night. There were instances when I would depart from advance fire bases and go in on foot. Once I was smuggled on a French merchant boat. In order to survive I used every instinct I had, everything my father taught me, and every lesson I learned in escape-and-evasion training and past months of combat experience. Typically extraction was on foot and there were instances where getting home took days. As I've said before, I was comfortable in the jungle, even when the going was hairy. While the circumstances were difficult, I can't say I wasn't proud of my success rate. I was a finite operator. If I went after a guy, he ended up dead.

Of course, taking out Viet Cong leaders and North Vietnamese government officials—like clearing a jungle trail of landmines and booby traps—wasn't exactly the blueprint for how to live a long life. Given the nature of the missions I was tasked with, it's a wonder I survived. Mostly, I think I was lucky. But I certainly wouldn't have made it out of Vietnam were it not for several of the Scouts. They were exceptionally courageous and tactically astute. Scouts were easily motivated and very well disciplined. I literally came to trust them with my life.

One publicized example of the Scout's earned reputation as exemplary fighters was Truong Kinh, who, during an eight-hour battle fighting with the Fifth Marine Regiment, killed thirty-one NVA. His exploits along with other successes of the Kit Carson Scouts became the stuff of military newspapers, for we wanted to publicize their actions and build momentum for expanding the program. My own exploits were, by contrast, the sort of thing only discussed on a need-to-know basis. Just enough leaked out that I picked up the moniker 007, which stuck—even following me into the cockpits of Northwest passenger jets in the years that followed. Even if I could discuss those missions in greater detail, I don't know that I have the capability, for memory of one melted into another and I've largely forgotten a great deal. Instead I only remember fragments, like dreams. I suppose that is the mind's way of suppressing memories that could only bring it harm.

By comparison, Kinh's bravery was reported widely and it deserved the acknowledgment it received. In a mission taking place just days after he was formally recognized as a Kit Carson Scout, Kinh first discovered six NVA hiding in rice paddies about thirty-five yards away. He shot four of the six, killing three. He then chased the other three and killed them, including an NVA officer. During a battle that raged over several hours, Kinh destroyed an enemy machine gun position—always a feared emplacement—with a grenade. He confiscated weapons and grenades from the dead in order to continue his attack, in one instance killing an NVA soldier, taking a grenade off his body, and throwing it thirty yards to kill another. He was also attributed with leading three wounded Marines to safety after they were pinned down by NVA fire. Marines fighting alongside Kinh credited him for guiding them through the battle zone, noting his uncanny ability to spot camouflaged VC they wouldn't have noticed, including those hiding in spider holes. I wasn't surprised. I'd been in action with Scouts enough times to know how ferociously they fought and how deeply they aligned with the "leave no man behind" spirit.

*

The battle experience and knowledge of VC tactics such as Kinh displayed were a large part of what made the Kit Carson Scouts so valuable. I learned to see the jungle differently by absorbing their knowledge. And when the real shit jobs arose, like needing a man to take a .45 and crawl into the moist, murky darkness of a VC tunnel in order to clear it, the Scouts were always the first to volunteer. When it came to tunnels, they were often the only ones who would fit through the narrow passages. Their heroics and their will to fight soon endeared them to the American Marines who fought alongside them.

Attrition rates were high for Scouts, yet they never shied from danger. It was in a tunnel-clearing operation that I lost one of my best, a reliable man named Theat. He was dragging a VC out of the tunnel opening when the bastard detonated a bomb. It killed Theat along with a Marine and it wounded eight more. Another VC that Theat had just pulled out of the tunnel used the blast as a distraction to make a run for it. He cleared the blast zone only for us to punch him full of holes. His death was a meager compensation for the loss of someone as brave as Theat.

I'd grown extremely close to Theat, so close in fact, that I'd made him a promise. After a particularly nasty mission, when we were safely back in Da Nang eating chow, he said to me, "I'm probably going to die doing this work. If I do, I want to go home. I want to be buried in my village so that I will always be close to my family." I consented.

When Theat was killed I vowed to myself that I would make good on his wishes. I was raised to believe that your word was your bond and I intended to keep my word. I used the influence of a chaplain who worked in Da Nang to help me arrange to have Theat's body embalmed. The chaplain was another Pennsylvania man who knew my mom. (Small world, huh?) Anyway, to have a Vietnamese soldier embalmed was an extremely unusual request and it raised a lot of eyebrows. I didn't really care what others thought. I had a promise to keep.

Then I put my other Scouts and CIA contacts to work so I could arrange a meeting with local Viet Cong. As odd as it sounds, such meetings happened more often than you might guess. That was part of the "wild west" nature of Da Nang. The VC were everywhere. Hell, sometimes we held events at an R & R facility run by the Navy, and the Viet Cong showed up in suits and bow ties. I guess they liked their booze and girls same as the next guy. Now, they didn't exactly advertise they were VC, no more than they did when they bribed shit-for-brains American contractors to let them onto base work details so they could aid sapper missions. Still, we couldn't move around Da Nang without assuming there were VC in our midst. Some we knew. And in the upside-down world of that war, even though the VC had a bounty on my head, we had a mutual respect for each other, aware of that unwritten code shared by warriors. Not that they honored any code unwritten or otherwise when they ignited a pick-up truck outside my barracks, but the code that I observed was to honor a dead man's request.

My contacts made good on their ability to arrange a meeting. In a jungle clearing outside of Da Nang, I used what Vietnamese I knew with a little French mixed in to convince a Viet Cong officer that I intended to transport Theat's body to his home village, well within disputed terrain and frequented by VC fighters. I told him that I wanted safe passage so that I could return a fallen soldier to his people. He agreed.

It wasn't the smartest mission I ever undertook, nor was it one that would have been supported by superiors if I worked within any sort of regular outfit. My two staff sergeants agreed to go with me so that we could trade off carrying Theat's body. It took the better part of four days to complete the trip. His family held a feast, or at least as much of a feast as they could muster, to honor their dead. We were honored that they invited us to attend.

It's the sort of story a lot of people don't believe. I don't hold it against them. Vietnam was filled with many things that didn't add up. I'm a math guy at my core. All my life I could do quick calculations in my head. I've always liked the precision of math the way I like the artful precision of a high-powered sniper scope or a well-made gun. One of the hardest things in my first weeks in Vietnam was learning that nothing was as it seemed. There was no definite math. The improbable became probable. To carry the embalmed body of a former VC through jungle terrain occupied by the enemy so that he could receive a proper burial ...such a thing could only happen in war, and maybe only in this war. Theat was killed in February of 1967. I'd been in-country for eleven months and had come to accept that nearly anything could be true.

Men like Theat helped level the battlefield because of their familiarity with the tactics of a guerrilla fighting force, its motivations, and its vulnerabilities. Perhaps if we had gone whole hog in adapting our own tactics or recognizing the fullest possible value of special forces operations, the war might have had a different outcome. We were fighting a different sort of enemy than we typically faced. Most officers were slow to learn from it. My experience equipped me well for a future most could not yet imagine.

The innovations and successes of the Kit Carson Scout Program did not go unrecognized. I was twice given commendations from General Westmoreland with the endorsement of General Walt, and at the end of my service in Vietnam I was awarded the Bronze Star, issued by V. H. Krulak, Commanding General of the Fleet Marine Force in the Pacific. Krulak had once overseen all counterinsurgency activities for the joint chiefs. Other bobbles that decorated my uniform by the end of my five years of service in the Marine Corps included the

Vietnamese Service Medal, the Air Medal (with three stars), the National Defense Service Medal, and the Republic of Vietnam Campaign Medal, alongside a Rifle Expert Badge and a Pistol Expert Badge. They did not include the two purple hearts I earned, one from having a Punji stick pierce my calf, the other from being hit by shrapnel that sliced through both knees. As I've explained, I declined the Purple Hearts for fear they might negatively impact my eventual application as a commercial pilot.

I carry scars as well as medals, both the literal and the metaphorical. I remain a light sleeper, reacting instinctively to the slightest sound or disturbance in the night. Otherwise I believe I returned largely unchanged by the war, although my wife at the time might say differently.

I had no idea that the rigorous training of Kit Carson Scouts or my time as a lethal assassin would prove every bit as useful throughout my career as a pilot during peacetime or in my graduating at the top of my flight class. Who would ever have guessed the extent to which I was trading one deadly adventure for another?

SAFE-CONDUCT PASS TO BE HONORED BY ALL VIETNAMESE GOVERNMENT AGENCIES AND ALLIED FORCES

Đây là một tấm Giấy
Thông Hành có giá trị
với tất cả cơ quan Quân
Chính Việt - Nam Cộng-
Hòa và lực lượng Đồng-
Minh.

Nº 314531 S

Left: PSYOPS
leaflet
Below:
Captain's stripes

Top row: Steve, 3
yrs old; Steve with
Fawn; at the
Golden Slipper
Camp.

Middle row: Steve
and his mom c.
1960; USMC 1962;
Vietnam 1966

Clockwise from top left: China Beach; 'Death card"; with the Northwest flagship747; Receiving the Behncke Award; in the "left seat"; Testifying before Congress

Clockwise from top left: 007; the Luckey family; Steve hunting; Steve and Jeannie travelling the world; "Cowboy Up"; Steve catching

Above left: Stephanie & Judd with Sarah & Megan, 1981. Right: Megan, Stephanie, Sarah; Below: Daughters with dad; prom night.

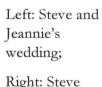

Left: Steve and Jeannie's wedding;

Right: Steve and Judd

Eyes Turned Skyward

"Flying is learning how to throw yourself at
the ground and miss."
—Douglas Adams, *Hitchhiker's Guide to the
Galaxy*

The first time I climbed inside a plane, I was hooked. When I was a kid, my dad often allowed me to go along when he accompanied a pilot hired by the state on fire spotting missions. Flying above the woods and mountains I'd known all my life was like seeing the world upside down. The sky opened before us. Below I could make out every river and stream. I could see the contours of land and the ridges and hollows. We soared so effortlessly. I wanted to replicate that feeling again and again. But as much as I loved being a passenger in that small airplane, I wanted the controls even then. My playtime fantasies flying in the World War II glider that Uncle Ernie brought to Promised Land were no match for the real thing, no matter how grand those dreams had been.

My fascination with flying goes back as far as I can remember. I cut up any magazine I came across with a picture of a plane in it so I could decorate my bedroom. One of my chief hobbies as a kid was building model airplanes. I had a big Piper Cub hanging from my ceiling. I loved everything about airplanes—their shape, their power, their sleekness. I thought they were sexy long before I had any idea what the word meant. But of course, it will come as no surprise that I loved their speed more than anything.

Almost as soon as I completed that first flight with my dad, I began to pester the pilot about how I could go about taking flying lessons. When I was a teenager, every free minute would find me at what is now Stroudsburg-Pocono Airport, taking classes to earn my pilot's license and putting in my flight hours. Flying felt as natural to me as tracking game or driving a car. I couldn't get enough. I was still in high school when I first soloed in a Piper Tri-Pacer. I was a unique sort of kid any way, but I was definitely the only odd duck I knew who carried a private pilot license before he had an ID that showed he was of legal age to buy beer.

That Piper Tri-Pacer mostly succeeded in making me want more—more time in the air, more speed, more adrenaline. I'd always had a need for speed. There was no one my age in Monroe County who drove faster cars than I did. A number of my uncles, and to a lesser extent, my dad, were gearheads. They'd find beat-up jalopies and work on them to see how fast they could make them go. In the winter we'd take our fastest car north to race across frozen lakes. In the summer it was dirt tracks. This was street racing, country style. There weren't rules, per se, short of some guidelines aimed at keeping you alive. It was all about who could build a car and then push it to its limits to get to the finish line first. Because I was more than a little bit crazy and because there is apparently truth to the saying that God protects fools and children (a premise I've tested throughout my life), I tended to do well in those races. The skills it takes to drive fast translate nicely to flying fast.

I also tended to drive fast even when I wasn't racing. It was important to me to own fast cars. I've held on to an "if you're not first, you're last" approach to life in general. Throughout high school and into college I worked (a lot, and in a lot of places)—in part to help out the family, in part to pay the tuition, and in large part to keep nice wheels under me. In addition to years working at the local market and summers at the gun range, I sold deer meat to local diners and, throughout college, I was employed as a bouncer at local bars like Chubs and Puzio's Square Bar. Like my parents, I was never afraid of work; it felt like a good payoff when it meant I had cash to drive the cars I desired, resources to customize them to my needs, and the ability to keep gas in the tank.

I've generally been a Chevy man. I still own a 1962 Corvette that I bought in the early 2000s that most everybody I know wants to buy from me. I was a full-time Montana resident then, and during many of those years the official state speed limit was "safe and prudent". That fit my personality perfectly.

Throughout my youth I drove Chevy Impalas, including the one I owned during college that I had to defend with a load of birdshot. That car was a modified '62 SS model, which I'd gotten a lead on because a family friend owned Gray Chevrolet. Chevy introduced the Impala with the Supersport option package the previous year, creating a true muscle car. That's the car that transported me to Officer Candidate School in Virginia and then on to flight school in Pensacola. Flying brought me to my first wife, Syble. I regularly flew into Brewton Field, an auxiliary training/landing facility for the Pensacola Naval Air Station, which happened to be near her home at the time.

Now, Syble's mom and I got along like two turds in a toilet bowl. Her name was Lodell; she and her boyfriend, Bill Rodgers, town manager of Brewton, Alabama, paid for our wedding and gave us most of the furniture for our first house. Lodell bought me my first pick-up. Bill even helped get me a side job as a deputy sheriff for Escambia County, my first official position in law enforcement, which came with "official" permission to drive fast. Lodell owned a business called Chemical Services and Supply, and because I was a licensed plumber and electrician, I worked for her a good deal when I didn't have obligations at the air station. Chemical Services and Supply was a legit business, and Lodell was a hell of a businesswoman—in large part because she seemed to know everybody in three counties. But she was knee deep in another kind of supply business, too—running moonshine—so Lodell understood the value of good drivers and fast cars. And I was a really good driver. You could sure move down a country road when you opened up that big V8, and the stronger springs and shocks of the SS package were really put to the test. Of course, the fact that I was running moonshine for Lodell one night and running a county patrol the next sort of gave me an advantage—a little inside scoop, if you will.

I never really saw the moonshine business as criminal enterprise, particularly not when there were *really* evil characters out there. Lodell and Syble learned the truth of that the hard way some ten years later when Syble's brother, Bobby, was murdered by the famous "Black Widow" killer, Judy Buenoano (at that time she used his last name, Morris). Bobby was a great guy. Throughout my year in Vietnam I'd rested more easily knowing that he was looking in on Syble daily, but he was clearly not a great judge of character when it came to that particular girlfriend. To be fair, she'd fooled others too—Judy was later convicted of killing her husband and another boyfriend, and she was believed to have killed a third romantic companion in addition to murdering her son. As you can imagine, Syble and Lodell both took Bobby's murder hard and carried the weight of their grief into other parts of their lives from then on.

But that all came later. Those years working for Lodell in the first half of the '60s were fun ones. I was twenty-three years old, a commissioned officer in the US Marine Corps, I flew jets for a living, and I drove moonshine as a paid hobby. I had the adventure of becoming a husband and then a father. Having a family kept me grounded, while flying jets and driving fast fueled my old habits. Those fit my competitive spirit, and competition among flight candidates is about as intense as it gets. Creating such an atmosphere is central to the way the military trains pilots, which, in turn, attracts a predictable type of personality. It's deadly work and to pull it off requires pilots who are confident and tested. I'd begun thinking about the military from an early age because it seemed the only way to a career in flying, and more important it was the only way to fly the fastest planes on the planet. Fulfilling my dream to fly would depend on an entirely practical matter: I needed to be the best.

When I entered the Marine Corps in 1963, Vietnam was in its early stages and the Air Force and Navy had nearly all of the pilot positions sewn up. If I went Army, I'd be stuck in helicopters. The Marines seemed like the only way for me to go.

And the only way for me to fly would be to become an officer, so I followed their game plan and joined the Marines as an air officer candidate. I had a four-year degree and had earned good marks. I'd already been flying on my own for more than a half dozen years. But as I drove that Impala to Officer Candidates School in Quantico, Virginia, I knew I needed to emerge at the top of my class in order to advance in flight training.

I did well enough there to be one of three who qualified for flight training, so it was onward to Naval Air Station Pensacola where I would fly out of Saufley Field as part of Training Squadron VT-1, or the Eaglets. There, in Aviation Preflight Indoctrination (API), we spent half the day in the classroom learning the academics of flight, including aerodynamics, aviation physiology, and meteorology. The other half of the day we learned the cockpit itself, practicing in simulators and learning crucial skills like water and land survival. The swim portion of training included learning survival strokes, mastering tactics of drown proofing, swimming a mile in a flight suit, and "riding the dunkers"—escaping from a simulated submerged plane. We learned how to build shelters, find fresh water, make animal traps and snares—things we'd need to do if we were shot down and in a survival situation, lessons that were already more than familiar to me.

The two candidates who entered API with me both washed out. I thrived and secured a move to Naval Air Station Whiting Field where I became a member of Training Squadron VT-6, the Shooters.

There we flew the T-28 Trojan, a trainer used to familiarize us with jet aircraft. Each new phase of training meant new challenges and more speed—exactly what I was seeking. I wanted to push myself to become the very best pilot I was capable of being. At Whiting I tallied several Student of the Week honors and was then awarded Student of the Month, which eventually led to Student of the Year. Because I finished at the top of my flight class, I was allowed to choose my pipeline. Obviously, I chose jets. Less than one percent of pilots got jets.

Success in the T-28 meant a move from Florida to Naval Air Station Kingsville in Texas. There, at long last, I got to live out my dream by strapping a jet engine onto my backside as part of my advanced flight training at VMFAT Marine training squadron. Much to my dismay that also meant time spent in the classroom again, but we soon moved on to flight simulators and then into the aircraft itself.

I thrived at Kingsville and completed my carrier qualification flying AF-9Js off the USS Lexington. Carrier operations bring air combat pilots to the pinnacle of their training. The AF-9J, a conversion of the F9F-8, was a single-seat attack fighter developed specifically for aircraft carrier deployment. It was a honey to fly—responsive and perfect for weapons training, especially with its twin cannons and a full bomb or missile payload; it was also capable of carrying two wing-mounted Sidewinder missiles. Before my training was complete, I was also certified on the A-4 Skyhawk and the F-11 Tiger.

As we advanced to state-of-the-art combat fighters, most of our training was in aerial dogfights; we were kind of like jet-propelled gunslingers at the O.K. Corral—just what I'd wanted since those days sitting in that flightless glider back at Promised Land. Dogfight training proved something I already knew in my gut before I ever started flying with the Marines: The best pilots are more than a little bit crazy. Our instructors created a highly competitive environment, designing every lesson to push us to our absolute limits. Whether we were dogfighting against them or against our fellow students, the very nature of the game was to force us to the lethal edge of our abilities. We were graded on every aspect of our training both in the classroom and in the cockpit. As in Pensacola, our scores were an aggregate reflection of performance in academics and also in the aircraft. Every take off, every landing, every maneuver, and every missile launch was graded. Because the stakes were so high— and higher still on an aircraft carrier—we were even scored on how we taxied. In the world of naval aviation, something as small as a brake failure after a successful landing could result in taxiing right off the ship or using another multimillion dollar airplane as an improvised chock block.

Sometimes it felt that we were being assessed even when off duty, and since pilots are notorious for being competitive in every aspect of their lives, we were constantly challenging one another to see who could drink the most, win the most bar fights, or gain the attention of the prettiest women. Mostly our instructors looked the other way when it came to such activities—even drunken fights. Choices that might seriously derail career opportunities for other Marines were largely ignored when they involved fighter pilots.

Those outside aviator communities often view fighter pilots as cocky, and in truth we probably were. There's a pecking order in the flying world, and just as the best, senior-most pilots in commercial aviation fly the biggest, best-engineered planes, fighter pilots stood head and shoulders above the others and rightly flew the fasted aircraft. Every bar near every military base with a flight training or pilot squadron has reserved seating for those who fly jets. We didn't have to say anything; we just knew the prime seats were reserved for us. They might as well have had our names stenciled on them the way that our planes did. That tends to feed one's ego.

We would need to be the very best once we got our wings and deployed, for in Vietnam dogfights happened regularly and they happened against our Cold War opponents. The Soviet Union supplied North Vietnam with pilots who served as instructors and who manned

most of their aircraft. They were experienced, well-trained pilots flying
state-of-the art equipment. Therefore, the goal of our flight school was
to graduate pilots who were superior to the Soviet's best.

Competing against the very best Marine aviators during
training also meant flying off of aircraft carriers. A lot of pilots feared
carrier training—and a lot bombed out. I thought it was the best thing
since sliced bread. If an aircraft carrier were any sexier, I could have
done away with women. I loved landing on a carrier. The worse the
weather, the better. Night landings? Piece of cake. But then, I think
I've established by now that I'm a little bit crazy. It takes real skill and
discipline to learn to land on a carrier. It doesn't help that the damn
decks are moving—pitching and bobbing on waves. But I thrive on
challenges, so when conditions were tough I wanted to prove that I
could meet their demands.

Carrier training started on land where a strip of runway was
white-washed in the exact dimensions of an aircraft carrier deck for
field mirror landing practice (FMLP). It began with practice on
touch-and-goes. Let me tell you, the deck of an aircraft carrier is
damn small. The first time I saw only 300 feet of white paint laid out
on a 2,000-foot runway, I wondered how I manage not to die. But
those skills became so well practiced that I eventually operated on
instinct and muscle memory. I *had* to learn to get it right. Carriers are
entirely unforgiving.

This is true in every aspect of a crowded flight deck at full
operation with aircraft rising from bays below deck, fuel trucks
scurrying back and forth, planes taxiing, aircraft taking off and landing,
and arresting cables slicing up and down the deck—it's all orchestrated
chaos. At any time a flight-deck operations seaman might be blasted
off the deck from the exhaust of a jet. For the pilot, the chaos hits full
throttle with the thrill of the catapult. The catapult system used on
carriers is capable of launching a plane from zero to 150 mph in two
seconds. It's kind of like being shot out of a gun, only as you exit the

barrel you've got about a thousand decisions to make. If you suffer mechanical failure or you've got the aircraft weight wrong and you don't make airspeed or maintain pitch, you've got to eject before the plane leaves the deck if you have any hope of surviving.

After succeeding in touch-and-goes, we progressed to landing the damn bucket-of-bolts by engaging arrester cables. This required mastering the precision of flight path and touchdown timing needed to catch the jet's tail hook in one of the cables. There are four of these on a carrier, and the best pilots hit the third one with consistency for it offered the most effective stoppage range and the smoothest landing of the four. (In reality, decelerating from 150 mph to a complete stop in seconds is never really something you'd describe as smooth.) By aiming for the third cable, you've still got a backup chance of catching the second or fourth in case of a miss. I don't even know why the first wire exists, because if you catch it you're clearly coming in way too low and are damn lucky you didn't hit the stern of the ship. Counterintuitively, when landing on a carrier you push the plane to full throttle as soon as you touch the deck, just in case you miss the arresting cables and have to "bolt"—to take off and circle around again for another attempt.

When that happens you become known as a "bolter". As if a pilot needed a reminder that being a bolter is a bad thing, one seat in the pilot ready room of every carrier has a seat with a bolt hanging above it. This is the room where pilots are briefed on mission parameters and objectives prior to takeoff and where every flight they take is reviewed after completion; so needless to say, you don't want to spend time in that seat. In a fighter-pilot ready room the best seat is reserved for the best pilot, just like at the bar.

Of course, just getting on and off the ship without crashing isn't the whole mission even if it is one of the toughest challenges in aviation. Dogfighting was serious business. When two aircraft are screaming toward each other at Mach 1, each with intent to take the other out of the sky, things can get dicey whether in practice or for real. There's no room for error. Decisions have to be made in milliseconds. There's a reason that training squadron classes are named after pilots who died in training. Pilots die with frightening regularity while training, whether in dogfight collisions, on takeoffs and landings, or through freak accidents or mechanical failures.

During my years of training as a Marine aviator, I had my own need for a "nylon letdown"—ejection with a parachute—after another student and I took each other's wings off in mid-air. I pulled that ejection handle and said my prayers. Unfortunately, the other student joined the ranks of those remembered only by a squadron call sign. Death is part of the nature of the business. When you're a fighter pilot, you know that any mistake could easily be a fatal one for yourself and for others. Such knowledge is among the unique aspects of the occupation. We might have been crazy in some ways, but we were stone serious about our work. Being a fighter pilot is perfect training ground for commercial aviation, for you become accustomed to carrying the tremendous weight of responsibility for other lives.

To succeed as a fighter pilot, you've got to find a way to balance cultivated intelligence with common sense, and competitive hunger with reasonable decision making. You have to love speed. You have to want to excel. You can't be easily rattled. And yes, you've got to be a bit crazy. In my case, I guess craziness paid off. The wings I earned at Kingsville in 1964 remain one of my life's proudest accomplishments.

Upon completion of flight training, I was stationed at Marine Corps Air Station Cherry Point in eastern North Carolina for attack pilot training courses and other specialty courses that would prepare me for flying in Vietnam. During this time Syble and I were married, and it wasn't long after that that Stephanie, the first of my children, came along. I was assigned to VMA Squadron 332 flying the A-4 Skyhawk, and shortly after completion of our training we were dispatched to Vietnam where I started my tour flying the sorts of missions we'd been trained for.

And then there were the ones we'd *not* been trained for. As I've shared, the need for fighter pilots had largely disappeared, and soon I was frequently assigned to other aircraft and other types of missions. During my first couple of months in Vietnam, I often flew surveillance missions to ascertain the location of enemy combatants. More often than was comfortable, these missions meant flying low and drawing enemy fire. We covered the same ground with enough regularity that, flying low and slow we could pick up on subtle changes in the terrain that indicated the presence of enemy. You had to look for the smallest signs and alterations because the jungle is adept at hiding enemy troop movement. Mostly I flew the Cessna O-1 Birddog on these kinds of missions, a plane that we relied on heavily for Forward Air Control despite its lack of armor. It wasn't my cup of tea, but I took the missions assigned to me and tried to do good where I could.

One day, I located an enemy encampment. I'd grown quickly adept at learning to read the jungle, something I attribute to my childhood passed in the woods. The North Vietnamese were impressive, moving long distances without being noticed and sometimes they'd pop up where you knew they hadn't been the day before. If you saw them at all, you'd think they were a mirage. The Birddog didn't exactly have a lot of firepower, and in fact, if the enemy decided to let loose on me it could make for a bad day, although mostly they didn't engage spotting aircraft because they didn't want to reveal their position. But I was equipped with three radios for air strike coordination and I knew we didn't have ground personnel in the immediate area, so I got on the horn and called in a strike. The Airborne Command and Control Center replied that they didn't have any available strike aircraft because they were all off bombing the hell out of other targets. I knew there was a battleship group within range and radioed in to see if they wouldn't train their big guns on the coordinates. They were tied up too, pounding someone else. "Well, hell, I thought, I've got a definite sighting on an enemy, no support, and no attack capabilities of my own." But I was flying so low that I saw movement down along the river near where I'd identified the enemy location. When I flew close, I saw it was a group of elephants. They were wallowing around in the mud like they were giving each other facials. The mud was kind of pink colored, and they were covered in it. I estimated the distance between the elephants and the enemy encampment, and thought, "Hell it's worth a shot."

It's been my experience that animals aren't enthusiastic about noisy mechanical objects coming in out of the sky at close range. Flying low and slow I took a vector that was likely to move the elephants up out of the river on a trajectory towards the encampment. I fired a smoke marker as I came in on them, and I opened my side window and laid down a strafing line with my M-16 behind them for good measure. That got them up and moving at a full run. The canopy over the enemy position was so thick that I couldn't really see if the stampede had the effect I'd hoped for, but who knows, maybe they took out one or two. I sure would have liked to have seen the looks on their faces if those elephants reached them.

When I returned to base, my flight commander asked me what I'd seen. I replied, "Elephants, sir."

"Is that so?"

"Yes, sir," I told him. "Pink elephants, sir."

I didn't hear the last of that one for a good, long while.

Those were the only pink elephants I saw in Vietnam, though, once the Marines curtailed my flying career as I've already shared, I saw plenty of other strange things.

Once I left Vietnam and then, with a good deal of reluctance, left the Corps, I still had a family to feed. Stephanie was less than two years old, and I'd missed most of the first year-and-a-half of her life.

Even in my early days with the Marine Corps I'd known that eventually I'd want to parlay my skills into a sustainable job, and one career on my radar was a commercial job in the airline industry. When a friend from my original squadron reached out to recruit me to fly for Northwest Orient Airlines, I jumped on it. That landed me in Minneapolis and into flight officer training.

As a military pilot and a Marine, I had little worry that I could ace training with Northwest. I had a reputation that preceded me from my experiences in Vietnam, and as a Marine aviator I also had the advantage of the Corps' larger reputation. In flying circles, if you were a Marine or Navy pilot you were known hands down as the best. You wiped your ass with the rest of the guys. I was surprised then, very early on, when I was pulled out of a ground school class by the head of Northwest personnel, a guy by the name of C. Randall Breezey. Breezey told me that there was a problem with my letters of recommendation. That confused me—I knew I had strong letters. It turned out that Breezey was accusing me of falsifying the letters. He told me that he didn't think they were real and that if I didn't come clean, I'd be done at Northwest before I'd ever started. I told him to call the signers of those letters. Angry at the accusation, I returned to class thinking Breezey was a total clown.

Later that week Breezey again pulled me out of class, summoning me to his office. I wondered if he was making good on his threat and that I'd be handed my walking papers. Instead he offered to buy me dinner.

"I'm sorry," he apologized. "I've never seen letters so full of praise, and given who they're from I thought you were trying to pull a fast one."

One of the letters was from General Lew Walt. The other was from General William Westmoreland, commander of US forces in Vietnam. I took Breezey up on his apology-by-way-of-steak. In the end, we became friends who would laugh at the memory of our first interaction.

After that hiccup I soared through all of the Northwest training. Like the atmosphere I'd known in VMFAT training onboard the Lexington, we were not only graded on every aspect of our actions but we knew we were in competition with one another to get into the best pilot squadrons. That, in turn, would mean a fast track to flying the best planes. I completed training and made my official debut as a Northwest pilot on December 4, 1967. I became Northwest pilot number 1329.

In commercial aviation, flying the best planes—which always meant bigger aircraft flying longer, more desirable routes with newer equipment—is directly tied to salary. To get a raise as a commercial pilot, one had to move up to a bigger plane. I'd naively thought I'd make captain in three years, but right after I was hired the economy soured and Northwest curtailed much of their hiring for nearly a decade. I ended up flying from the copilot's seat for thirteen years as a result.

I was anxious to move up. Some of the captains I flew with were fantastic and some were controlling. I always tried to make the cockpit a fun place. The flight attendants liked to come up to the cockpit and they'd spend time in the observer's seat, flirting and revealing their long legs and ask for stories or swap gossip. We had serious work to do, but I've got a playful personality. That meant I developed some important friendships. But I also alienated a few crusty old captains because I'm not the sort to take shit from people. I recall a bit of fun I had with one old salt.

We were on a layover in Taipei, flying a cargo route. It was the kind of duty I was ready to be done with—long international flights to Tokyo and Hong Kong and similar destinations. I was on a crew with a crusty old captain, an Englishmen who worked out of Minnesota on a US green card and with David Williams, a good friend who was our first officer. I'd come to know Taipei well. Hanging around after dinner, I told David, "Let's go by some fake watches." Taipei was famous for its black market. David was curious and up for a bit of adventure. He didn't know a lot of guys around the airline because he'd been furloughed for the last eleven years. We got along well and shared a lot of the same interests. A former Navy pilot, we were kindred spirits. I enjoyed him and had fun introducing him to some of the quirkier bits of international travel.

It was after midnight, and pitch black because in those days they turned off all the lights in Taipei. I navigated the city streets to a clandestine store I knew. I didn't let on because I was getting a kick out of watching David try to make sense of what we were doing. Outside the store was the owner's wife. She was on the sidewalk, cooking rice. She saw our uniforms and pointed for us to go inside. There we found her husband manning the counter of what had the appearance of a convenience store. I told him we there for watches. He nodded and moved a cabinet out from the wall to reveal a little door. We had to stoop down to pass through the door. It opened into a bigger room loaded with boxes. The proprietor returned the cabinet to its position and closed the door behind him and began laying out all kinds of fake Rolex watches. David was in amazement and falling for every line the guy was selling him. I bought a couple of watches for shits and giggles, and David bought several. He had teenage kids and knew they'd have a lot of fun wearing these flashy watches to school even if the fake gold gilding would wear off in three months. He sold them for ten bucks a pop, but they looked like the real thing. We came out with a dozen. The store owner placed them neatly in a little velvet bag like we'd bought real jewelry.

The next day we were in the cockpit flying back to the US, and David brought out the bag to admire our purchases. The captain saw the watches and got all riled up. "That's contraband," he said. "You can't bring that back to the States."

He got more and more worked up. We'd come to hate the guy. He was an alcoholic who was now on the wagon. Sober, he'd turned into a real asshole. Back when he was drinking, he was a hell of a nice guy, and our only objection then was that he'd come on board hungover, would curl up on the observer's seat and go sleep eight or ten hours, abandoning us to do all the work. Now he stayed at the controls but was absolutely no fun to be around. As he got amped up over the watches, he said, "If customs finds contraband on our flight, they're going to pull my green card and send me back to England. David and I exchanged a look and then I said, "Well, that wouldn't be a bad deal for us." That really pissed him off, and he stormed out of the cockpit saying he had to use the head.

I told David to give me the bag of watches. Our bags were in the cockpit behind our seats. I had the plane on autopilot, got up, unzipped the captain's suitcase, and stuffed the velvet bag down underneath his underwear. The captain returned with a cup of coffee and didn't say one word to us the rest of the flight.

We got to New York where we had to go through the pilot's line for international customs and agricultural clearance. The captain went through the line first. We hung back, but he stayed there a long time and had quite a conversation with the agent, who was looking at David and I the whole time. The captain didn't even have to put his bags on the counter for inspection and was waved on through. David went next, and the agent demanded that he put his bags on the counter and then proceeded to complete a thorough inspection before stamping his form and waving him through. Then he did the same thing to me. When he came up empty, the agent gave the captain a crusty look. The captain appeared perplexed.

Outside, waiting for the transport shuttle, I told the captain, "Excuse me, bub, I just need to get something out of your luggage." Then I bent down, unzipped his bag, felt around, and pulled out the bag full of watches. The captain went into a war dance there on the crowded JFK sidewalk, screaming obscenities, while David and I couldn't stop laughing.

I suppose you could say that irritating your senior officers wasn't a good promotion plan, but I couldn't pass up the opportunity for a little fun. The reality was that advancement in a union environment was always based on a blend of ability and seniority. I was an excellent pilot, and as the industry became profitable and I put in my time, my career advanced. I ended up flying for Northwest for thirty-three years, retiring in 2000 (in those days, mandatory retirement came at age sixty). I flew every aircraft Northwest had in its fleet and I became a trainer on nearly all of them. I ended my career with Northwest flying the left-hand seat of the 747-400, the very best plane in the fleet—air conditioning and cruise control were standard— logging routes mostly to Asia and Europe.

I remain appreciative of my long career with Northwest. I flew with fine colleagues and I had good relationships with both union officials and company bigwigs. At separate points in my life I was married to two Northwest flight attendants. My closest friend was a fellow captain with Northwest. Peter Reiss and I downed many a breakfast at a table that might as well have been reserved for us at the pilot center in Tokyo. We compared notes and swapped stories. Peter was active on the security committee for the airline and we often shared ideas on how to improve the nascent field of airline security. I enjoyed my career. But the simple truth was that I found most of the flying to be boring. Most people can't understand what I mean, but as cool as it is to fly a commercial jetliner, it just isn't the same as flying inverted at 1,000 miles an hour along a railroad track with your tail a few feet off the ground. There isn't a lot of room for crazy in commercial aviation.

Yet it was a rewarding career if not always an exciting one. But then I guess "exciting" is relative, for not only did I fly a 747 with a cruising speed of 570 mph, but every week I woke up in London and

Paris, or Tokyo and Hong Kong. Early in my career, always up for a challenge, I loved flying into airports the other pilots hated, mostly because they were difficult places to land. That's how I first started flying into Montana, the state that eventually became my home. I hit most of the Montana airports in the early years when young pilots drew the less glamorous regional routes. That meant flying into places like Butte, which sits in a hole, making it a damn difficult place to land. It's the sort of airport—just what I liked—where you either stuck your landing or you busted your ass. Plus it was a fun town. The old mining community was still a bit of a lawless place in those days, which was just my speed.

I started flying during an age when, although dangerous because of terrorism and political hijackings, it was an industry that was still seen as glamourous. Many people couldn't afford to fly, so they associated flying with what they saw in the movies and on television, and they assumed that those who flew, like those who did the actual flying, lived adventurous, exciting lives. Many pilots lived up to the stereotype. In truth, a lot of pilots were brash and dashing, nearly all coming out of combat flying experience, and flight attendants were selected because they were slim, attractive, and gregarious. Crew members mostly enjoyed one another and we often continued those friendly exchanges in social settings. It was a time when layovers were pleasant because we were in good company. If we wanted a party, they weren't hard to find. A lot of pilots drank more than they should have and drank closer to their report times than some of us would've liked. Flying around the world, often into glamorous locations where tourists were living out their fantasies, flight crews frequented places where people behaved in ways that might make their mothers blush.

For many, travel offered a break from ordinary life. This was especially true for those who could afford to fly. Passengers were granted superior service. During the first half of my career the flying public was small and passengers received a lot of amenities. Every airline was competing for business, and regional carriers still thrived. People dressed up to travel, not just in accordance with the times but because flying was viewed by most as an exotic adventure. Planes had full bars on board and the booze flowed freely. Passengers were served hot meals on real plates and they were provided actual utensils. Kids were invited into the cockpit and were enthusiastic to meet their pilots.

In those early years the aviation community was small and intimate. You knew most of your crews and they knew you. Your reputation was everything and it always preceded you. If you were known for being good to work with and good at your job, your crew responded with respect and a willingness to make the flight pleasurable for all. People around the industry knew who the best pilots were. And they knew which pilots treated them well and were fun to hang around with off duty. There was a camaraderie among Northwest employees that made it a great place to fly.

Naturally we had our squabbles—both as crews on the plane and employees of the corporation. As in any industry, there were grumpy old-timers and those who didn't really pull their weight, like those who slept their way across the Pacific. Strikes were not uncommon and sometimes the labor negotiations were tense and overly long. Scabs were always an issue and remained a source of further problems once the strikes were over. Early in my career there were downturns and layoffs as well as strikes, which meant that as a young junior pilot I scrambled to cover bills. That was one reason I stayed current in law enforcement training and secured a reserve deputy position in Hennepin County. It helped pay the bills and gave me an outlet for my wilder side. There's nothing like chasing bad guys to get your adrenaline up. When contracts were secure, profits were up, and flying was regular, the nature of a pilot's schedule still allowed me to get in some shifts with the sheriff's office.

Further augmenting my livelihood, I also ran a gunsmithing shop for a number of years. And because of the training I'd completed with the FBI, I spent a lot of hours flying to the scenes of hijackings to aid investigations—sometimes internationally. Needless to say I was more than a little bit busy during that period. By the time I'd hit twenty years flying with Northwest, I'd been married twice and had four children. I owned a house in Montana that I built myself and another in Minneapolis/St. Paul. It was an active lifestyle.

At its center was flying. As with shooting, most of what came my way arrived because of my reputation as a pilot. I'd been trained by one of the most elite aviation forces in the world. I was good at what I did. One opportunity led to another, including those that arose from my daily flights and my understanding of the industry's needs that others either couldn't see or wouldn't voice. But my reputation was also advantageous in smaller ventures such as outfitting and guiding hunters. When I started that pursuit all I had to do was post a notice on the cork board in Minneapolis and within hours I'd have a full group of interested pilots signed up.

As it was when I was a little kid cutting pictures of airplanes out of magazines to pin up around my room, flying is the sort of thing that grabs you by the short hairs and doesn't let go. I flew for fun even when I flew for a living. My daughter Sarah recalls a time when she was seventeen or eighteen and I took her and her sister Megan up in my friend's biplane. At that time we were living in Manhattan, Montana, and I deadheaded in and out of the airport in Bozeman. Turned out that my buddy had his biplane hangared there and he offered to let me take it out, so I thought I'd give the girls a thrill. It was a two-seater with the pilot in the rear, so the girls took turns while I ran them through a series of barrel rolls, stalls, and banks. Those little planes will do just about anything you ask of them; you feel connected to their every movement in a way that the shear speed of a modern fighter or the bulk of a commercial carrier can't replicate. We filled up every inch of the sky. The girls didn't quite know what they signed on for, but they loved every minute of it despite their fear and their new experience of pulling G's. The next day, Sarah told me that kids at her school were talking about some crazy guy flying above their campus like he was putting on an airshow.

It's been years since I have flown. But I still drive fast cars.

Luckey, Steve Luckey

"Oh, I travel ... a sort of licensed
troubleshooter."
—James Bond, from *Thunderball*

I don't remember exactly when I first got the nickname 007. I think it probably dates all the way back to Vietnam. The James Bond movie *Thunderball* came out the year before I landed in-country in 1966, and Bond was incredibly popular among the troops. They were, after all, overwhelmingly young men who dreamed of lives filled with women, intrigue, fast cars, and a clear division between bad guys and good guys. I had a few years on most of my fellow Marines, but I wasn't so different from them in wanting such things. What set us apart was that while they watched movies, I lived out parts of that 007 fantasy. Not so much regarding women or fast cars, but mostly the espionage and secretive, high-stakes missions. I took part in missions typical of the American experience in Vietnam, from flushing Viet Cong out of villages to participating in major division-sized engagements. On the other hand, missions that required me to spend time among spies for Israel's Mossad, the Korean Central Intelligence, and the CIA transcended top-secret classification.

With access to General Walt's Level 6 (secret and high risk) security clearance, I had my share of adventurous Bond-like expeditions while in Vietnam, utilizing helicopters, submarines, and parachutes to reach targets behind enemy lines. Parachuting alone—in the middle of the night and into jungle terrain likely filled with enemies—most definitely feels like something out of a movie. As does swimming out of a submarine's torpedo tube.

Surreal experiences weren't limited to modes of transportation. Probably because of my success in developing the Kit Carson Scouts, I found myself invited more and more often to dinners, mixers, and similar events throughout Da Nang. These soirees were attended by an odd array of Americans, Vietnamese, and internationals. I'd come to know a few individuals—Christians-in-Action types—who I felt I could trust, but at these gatherings there were any manner of spooks (Christian or otherwise), few that I could actively identify as CIA, though many probably were. All dropped information. But such intelligence never came in straight lines. I'd get a piece here, a hint there, a photograph passed, or an invite for another meeting. Some were connected with the United States Agency for International Development (USAID) and other relief organizations, some with the USO, but most were with private contractors and security consultants or embassy staff. Of course, the best measure of any intelligence operative is the degree of clandestine success he—or she—had. Most of the time I was chasing shadows in the dark.

But inevitably, as one piece of information connected with another, I'd receive a name and a photo along with the time and the place where I was supposed to be. From there I'd join up with special forces personnel or operatives from any of a number of international intelligence organizations—the Korean Central Intelligence Agency, the French Service de Documentation Extérieure et de Contre-Espionnage, the Mossad—and then I might find myself strategically dropped on top of a mountain or parachuting into the dark. I found out facts I would never have otherwise known. Like that because there were still diplomats flying in and out of Hanoi even at the height of the war, a plane with the right electronic signature and silhouette on the proper flightpath could be viewed as not worthy of notice, so much so that you could find yourself in remote places in the far north where no one would expect an American Marine, a weapon, and a name on a hunting tag.

I count the dedicated experts of the Korean Central Intelligence Agency and the Mossad as my teachers. They were the best in the world, and I learned well. The Koreans were extremely effective and particularly ruthless. They understood something that we in the West have taken a lot longer to learn. They were familiar with insurgents and terrorists for decades before Americans were. As a result, they understood that, because guerillas followed no rules of engagement and often employed the tactics of terrorists, the typical codes of conduct didn't work with them. As a result, the Koreans used what some would see as extreme measures, such as the helicopter interrogation where two bad guys go up in a helicopter, one is pitched out an open door and then the interrogator suggests to the remaining guy that he might want to start talking. With the kinds of hardcore Viet Cong we encountered, I saw the value of such approaches.

Of course, around the world most in intelligence services regard the Mossad as the premier espionage agency in the world. Their relentless pursuit of targets and the sophistication of their intelligence and covert abilities were legendary. I was lucky enough to count several Mossad agents as teachers and friends over the years. It is a brotherhood that never leaves you. I recall one time, decades after Vietnam when I was on a layover in Berlin. I was walking to dinner one night with two fellow crew members and a black Audi with heavily tinted glass pulled alongside. A window rolled down and an accented voice shouted, "Steve Luckey!" The car was loaded with Mossad agents in town for a security conference. They were heading off for the evening's extracurricular activities, which invariably involved lots of booze and attractive women. "Get in," they said, in a fashion my crew members told me the next day that they found sinister. I offered a quick apology to my colleagues and was whisked away for a night of partying. When I arrived at the airport the next morning, hungover and having barely slept, my crewmates told me excitedly that they didn't think they'd see me again and hadn't known if they should file a report with the German Polizei. I chuckled, brushed their concern aside, and told them, truthfully, that they were just old friends.

While some of my missions in Vietnam were in the company of Mossad or Korean agents, more typically, I was alone. And inevitably, following scant directions, I'd discover an immaculate villa or some other anomaly in the midst of what seemed the most remote part of the jungle I could ever imagine. There, left largely to my own devices, I would carry out the work I'd been directed to do and then find my way back to safety. I was tasked to do what I was good at—shoot. In the course of any action, circumstances could easily shift. I made spontaneous decisions; a lot of what the CIA and others were doing seemed to be made up on the fly. They probably were. This wasn't Eastern Europe or even Hong Kong. It was a war within a war in a place we knew almost nothing about. A lot of what I was asked to do hadn't been done before. We were writing books that had never been before written. Often upon my return, General Walt would congratulate me on a job well done without ever quite acknowledging what the job had been. He once told me, "I'll always have your back if push comes to shove, but otherwise it's better if I didn't know any details."

I woke up most days thinking I was dreaming. When you're placed into a world that seems cinematic, it's a hard thing to get your head around. My training with special forces helped, of course, but there's a moment—like when you're about to step out of a plane into a dark night sky—that feels more than a little surreal, a little 007.

Unlike Bond, I seldom had the equivalent of a "Q" equipping me with fancy gadgets. And there wasn't exactly a bevy of blue-eyed beauties feeding me intelligence. On the other hand, I experienced my share of only-in-the-movies adrenaline rushes, and I did find prostitutes to be excellent sources of information. I became more than familiar with a cast of shady characters who seemed to come straight off a Hollywood set. It was through work with the CIA that I met one of my most important information sources and one of my significant Vietnamese friends, Vo Cong. Vo wore the uniform of an ARVN officer, but he'd been an American intelligence asset before the war was even a war. Fortunately he survived the conflict and fled the country at the war's end, becoming one of the widely known "boat people" who later made a life for himself and raised his family in Southern California. I considered him an American hero, even if he wasn't American at the time.

Acting on intelligence information supplied by others like Vo, I quite literally had a license to kill. The enemies I was directed to kill in Vietnam weren't just troublemakers and power brokers intent on causing disruption and causalities; they were bad men responsible for countless deaths. I was frequently employed as a "terminator", responsible for taking out targets identified by my superiors as requiring removal. Once General Walt gave the thumb's up, I was left to my own devices to solve the problem of the moment. At other times, I was asked to address problems that traditional means couldn't rectify effectively.

I remember General Walt dispatching me to the Hue Citadel one time because there was a group of snipers knocking the shit out of our helicopters. I deployed to the location and I took them out, one by one. They were good, but I was better. Years of hunting helped prepare me, and learning alongside the celebrated men of the 1st Marine Division Sniper Platoon up on Hill 55 took that training to the next level, cementing the discipline needed to hunt down those who were hunting me.

One famous combatant of Hill 55 was Carlos Hathcock, the deadliest sniper of the Vietnam War with ninety-three confirmed kills. Estimates suggest he was probably responsible for at least 300 more. I'd met Carlos at Camp Perry where he was an instructor. He'd won the Wimbledon Cup shooting championship in 1965, then reported to

Vietnam the same year I did in 1966. We were cut from the same cloth and shared very similar childhoods, shooting from an early age.

Known as White Feather for the feather he always wore in his bush hat, the Viet Cong placed a $30,000 bounty on his head. His reputation grew when he killed a Viet Cong patrol leader we'd nicknamed Apache because she so liked to torture American soldiers before she killed them, cutting away their eyelids as souvenirs and often castrating them, then leaving them to bleed to death. Her habit was to commit such torture within earshot of a base's perimeter wire so that the other Marines would have to hear their comrade's suffering. Hathcock hunted Apache for months before he finally got his chance. He identified her while he was pursuing a Viet Cong patrol when, at 700 yards, he saw one of them step off the trail and squat to pee, which signaled the target was a woman. He severed Apache's spine with his first shot.

Because Hathcock had such a bounty on his head (can I admit that a part of me was jealous that his bounty was so much larger than mine?) the North Vietnamese sent their best sniper, a guy who'd been given the moniker The Cobra, to hunt him down. Those two did quite a dance. On the day Hathcock finally bagged him, The Cobra had gotten a close shot off, likely only missing because Hathcock tripped on a log and the shot hit his spotter's canteen. Over many hours the two snipers circled one another until they had completely exchanged positions, orienting The Cobra toward the sun which glinted off his scope. Hathcock put his shot right through the scope.

Training with Hathcock and with the other snipers of the 1st Marines, I'd learned all the tricks needed to be successful, even in a setting like the one where he'd killed The Cobra. Believe me when I tell you that you learn to live with your butt in a permanent pucker when you're playing cat and mouse with another sniper. Up at the Hue Citadel I came out on top. I was a finite operator. My exploits aren't known in the way Hathcock's stories have entered the public domain, but then a lot of the kills I made exist in a world that falls off the books of any public record.

The requirements of my job during the war were highly unusual. Not many Americans were trained or sanctioned to do what I did. Killing another human being is not an easy thing to be responsible for. Going around adjusting the gene pool isn't psychologically healthy and not the kind of profession that's conducive to sleeping at night. Some things bothered me. I'm not the sensitive type, but I'm human. And the reality was that I spent a lot of years doing such work long after I left Vietnam. There's a lot I can't say about missions that I completed for the CIA and the FBI during the decades following Vietnam, not only because of the nature of that work but because of the security clearance I was granted. Suffice it to say that my "real" life as a commercial airline pilot offered plenty of good cover for extracurricular travel. With a day job that took me around the planet and a history of taking "unique" actions, I was pretty attractive to those who work in the darker worlds that we like to think only exist in spy novels. There's a lot that happens behind the scenes in order to keep our country safe that doesn't get advertised, and for good reason.

There's one aspect of the job that spy novels don't spend enough time developing. When you do black ops work, you become obsessed with protecting your actual identity, even to the point of distancing yourself from it. The people you love can easily become vulnerable if they truly know what you do. They also become a means to access you should you become a target. For the safety of people closest to you, you're forced to lie to them and to withhold a great deal. Trying to balance a normal life and career with a secretive one is kind of like trying to stay astraddle an unbroken horse. You never know when you'll get bucked off.

Hiding so much of your life takes a psychological toll as well. Along with secrets comes emotional distance. And with such distance comes unintended harm. As a result, I "retired" from clandestine work more than once. I did so somewhat formally in the 1980s after eleven years. I knew it was time to get out. I'd pushed to the edge way too often; the deeper I got into the darker and grittier sides of securing a democracy, the more it felt like my soul belonged to the devil. I prefer controlling my own destiny. As you've probably guessed by now, there's a part of my personality that's capable of slipping over the line, so I was smart enough to put my abilities to use in other, less lethal ways. But there were still occasions when old contacts from prior cases came knocking for help even after my retirement. I couldn't deny them—I had spent years chasing people responsible for the deaths of countless others, so I remain committed, no matter the loss of sleep, psychological damage, or other prices paid. In one instance I chased an elusive target for decades, and when that target resurfaced I was called out of retirement in order to enact a different sort of "retirement". His.

While there's a lot I cannot discuss, I can say this: I can look back on my life—in Vietnam and out—and know that anyone I've let the air out of more than deserved the deflation. Those guys were problems looking for a solution. All my life, if I've been anything, I've been a problem solver. A troubleshooter.

Among my "not-fit-for-public-disclosure" work alongside federal law enforcement and intelligence operatives, I did encounter a real-life "Q". Paris Theodore was a former CIA contractor (one rumored to be a contract assassin) turned gadgeteer and firearms maker. Paris was a flamboyant character who loved to cloak himself in mystery. He wore his curly hair long and dressed the part of a 60s man of intrigue, wearing tight dark turtleneck sweaters and expensive shoes. To see him, you might think he was auditioning for a villain's role in a Bond film.

By the mid-1970s he was best known for his company Seventrees Ltd, manufacturer of easily concealed, quick-release holsters loved by FBI and CIA agents. Theodore's holsters were perfect for plainclothes agents and undercover operatives, but his real baby was the ASP which he began developing in 1966. The ASP was a pocket-sized pistol based on the Smith & Wesson Model 39 automatic.

Seventrees was a clandestine company hidden in plain sight on the 17th floor of a manufacturing building at 315 W 39th Street in the Garment District in Manhattan. Because Seventrees also served as a black ops center for the feds and because my 007 reputation didn't end with Vietnam, I came to know those offices—and Theodore—well.

The ASP was the perfect gun for close range situations, exactly the sort of operations Paris himself was involved in during his years with the CIA. The ASP featured many innovations that were entirely novel in its day and were soon copied by other small gun makers, including clear grips—a modification enabling the user to see the number of remaining unfired rounds; the guttersnipe—a gun sight designed for fast-instinct aiming that featured a beveled groove rather than a raised sight (making the gun less likely to hang up when making a quick draw out of a holster); and a forefinger grip on the trigger guard—today a standard feature of most modern handguns. I shot the weapon on several occasions, and it was the right tool for the right job—a thing that could only be designed by someone who'd experienced the "right job". Having trained in close-range weapons use, I appreciated the intelligent design of the ASP. Interestingly, John Gardner, who'd succeeded the original James Bond novelist Ian Fleming in 1984 with his book *Role of Honour,* replaced Bond's Walther PPK with an ASP.

Theodore operated out of a suite of rooms hidden behind a large vault in the back of the leather shop where he manufactured Seventrees holsters. The leather shop, an actual enterprise that logically attracted law enforcement types, served as perfect cover for

Paris's gunsmithing operation. It was mostly after hours that the place really came to life, and then it became hard for the regular employees to get their work done because they were always maneuvering around spies.

In 1980, Theodore formed Techpak, a company created to market a combat handgun shooting technique he had developed, which he called "Quell." The Quell system included things we're accustomed to in real law enforcement practice, as well as in movie depictions—a shooter's stance with weight balanced on both feet and a two-hand grip. He also developed human-cutout targets. Instead of placing a bullseye over the center of the chest, Paris used multiple targets placed on vital areas of the central nervous system, such as the spine, the head, and the medulla oblongata at the base of the skull. These were impact points that would fully incapacitate or immediately kill a human target. The concept of a "Quell stop" became standard training for many police departments and special agencies throughout the world. The Quell system was ideal for training to shoot in a hostage situation. When hostages were taken, almost always at close-quarter gunpoint, it was crucial to make pinpoint shots into the brain of the perpetrator. The objective was twofold: instant termination of the target, and striking elements of the brain that make a terrorist's muscles release his grip on a weapon or bomb trigger rather than involuntarily fire the gun or device.

Since guys like Paris Theodore seem like they belong in a novel or on a period Hollywood set, I'm at risk of being seen the same way. There's actually not much of this 007 segment of my life that I can comfortably share. Offering details about events or the names of targets could either endanger people who are still alive or it could reignite political tensions best left in the past. Most of this part of my life is known only to me and to those I directly worked with, many of who are no longer here. Even my family doesn't know the depth of my involvement, and they certainly didn't at the time. But

I'll share one story that still makes me laugh; it reveals the bizarre but vital aspect of the Quell stop approach for precisely targeted shots. It may reveal a little bit more as well.

As I've said elsewhere, my reputation from Vietnam tended to precede me, particularly among my colleagues at Northwest Airlines. What people knew—or thought they knew—of my time in Vietnam was really only a limited perspective of more complicated stories. Such intrigue didn't end with Vietnam, though. People knew I had a relationship with Mr. Nyrop and there was speculation as to why that was the case. But one particular story involved several Northwest employees, and so it quickly spread through the company grapevine. I was young enough to still be working my way up the ladder, mostly flying as first officer on domestic flights. On one sortie into La Guardia, I was saddled with a captain that I knew to be a crotchety old bastard. The flight crews didn't care for him much. He liked to exert his authority and could be a real blowhard and bully.

During that routine flight the navigator and I passed the time swapping stories—as I've admitted before, I'm not exactly short on the gift of gab. I don't even remember what we were talking about, but apparently it was enough to set the captain off. At one point he turned to me and said, "Luckey, you're so full of shit. I don't believe any of this crap people say about you."

I told him that I was sorry that he felt that way.

"I don't know who you're trying to fool," he said.

I informed him that during our overnight layover in New York I planned to visit some of the people I'd worked with; I then invited him to come along to see for himself that I wasn't pulling anyone's leg. The navigator became excited at the prospect and said he wanted to come along. I told him he was welcome. He challenged the captain to take me up on my offer as well, and finally the captain agreed, saying that at least "We can put this shit to rest."

The next day the three of us, along with a flight attendant I knew well, ventured down to the Garment District. The captain grumbled the whole way.

"What in the hell are we doing here?" he muttered as we got out of the taxi. "I don't know why you're hauling us into a warehouse."

I found the whole thing to be funny and I made the most of it. We took the elevator up to the 17th floor and into Seventrees. The captain was about to lose it, bitching about not needing any leather. He accused me of taking him on a snipe hunt.

"You're crazier than I gave you credit for, Luckey," he said.

I took my little group on through the shop, beyond the vault, and toward another door. The Seventrees employees barely gave us a second look; they were accustomed to all manner of people more interested in the unofficial activities of the shop.

When I opened the door into the restricted area, we were met by two men carrying machine guns. That got the old captain's attention and an exchange of looks among my companions. The men asked for my identification. I showed them my FBI credentials and they gestured me in. I told them that the others were with me. The men shrugged— they were mostly there for effect. The anteroom we'd entered was a kind of showcase for work federal law enforcement researchers were involved with. Paris had a flare for the dramatic, thus the machine guns as well as the showroom featuring wax heads attached to tall poles like a perverse art installation. Each head displayed clear evidence of a bullet entry wound.

The captain looked as though he might puke. "I don't know what kind of sick joke you're trying to pull, Luckey."

I calmly explained. "These heads are part of important research we're conducting to study the effect of precisely placed bullet wounds. Each display is an exact replication of an actual kill. We've been studying the biomechanics of how the body reacts when shot in critical nervous systems. In our line of work, we need to know when a kill shot will make a target release muscle control instead of constricting their muscles. That can be the difference between someone who has taken a hostage dropping a gun instead of pulling the trigger."

The captain's face was ashen.

"Come on," I told him, knowing I had him where I wanted him. "Let's see if anybody's around." I then took him into an office where a law enforcement colleague was working at his desk. I made introductions all around and we chatted for a bit. The captain looked as if he was searching for a way out of the building and back into a cockpit where he could feel in control. He scanned the office, his eyes settling on a number of pictures mounted on the wall behind the desk. They depicted images of men posing beside dead bodies. His glance kept returning to one picture in particular.

At last, stammering, the captain pointed at the picture and said, "The guy in that picture looks a lot like you."

"That's because it *is* me," I told him.

He removed himself from that office and back through the shop like his tail was on fire. He never said another thing to me about being tired of my stories. Funny thing: I never had to serve as his copilot again.

Over the years I've gotten a good laugh thinking about that layover adventure. I don't know what versions of the story may have been passed along among Northwest crews. I would guess its retelling was a bit like the game of phone tag we played as kids, but a few of my closest friends have heard the story directly from me. Whether the many versions share similarities, I can't know. There were other stories, of course, several with scenarios like traveling incognito within a foreign country and that sort of thing. The rest I leave up to your imagination. All in all, if I could share such stories, they might just make a good script for a Bond movie.

A good laugh was a welcome thing. Exotic notions of espionage are best left for novels and movies where you can live out your fantasies—the real thing isn't nearly as glamorous. It isn't a lot of fun lying to people you care about. And those who choose to serve, whether in the military, in law enforcement, or in clandestine services, will likely experience a number of things that shouldn't be talked about anyway. No good would come of it. When your job requires you to fire weapons at living targets, it doesn't matter if you do it up close or at a distance, in the chaos of a battlefield or within the silence of a sniper scope—at the end of the day you alone are left to face your demons and to speak for your actions.

But lives are saved because of such actions. In a world that most aren't privy to, there's not a lot of room for philosophical ponderings regarding the question: When is taking one life a warranted exchange for saving an exponential number of others? In the end, someone has to do the hard work. I was asked to answer a call. I would do it again if asked.

Menacing Skies

"I'd gladly stand up next to you and defend
Her still today . . ."
—Lee Greenwood, "God Bless the USA"

When you buckle into the pilot's seat of a commercial jetliner, you are profoundly aware that every life on board is in your hands. It's an awesome responsibility. I would never initiate a preflight procedure without mentally registering that fact. One of the ironies of a pilot's job, however, is that it demands that your full attention be focused in front of you—on the instrument panel, the controls, and whatever's beyond the windscreen—yet passengers for whom you're responsible are seated beyond a closed cockpit door behind you. Among them, also within your responsibility, are any and all threats. If a passenger decides to attack the cockpit, whether as a terrorist intent on bringing down the plane, a hijacker intent on using the plane as ransom, or a passenger in the midst of a psychotic episode or just having a bad day (or one too many drinks), you're never going to see him coming.

To be aware of such threats was a main training objective when I began my career with Northwest. As I've discussed, hijackings at gunpoint or with the threat of a bomb were rampant in the late 1960s and early '70s. Only months removed from combat, my mind was already operating on high alert; transitioning to a cockpit where I needed to be aware of every detail of the plane's status as well as passenger behavior was probably a blessing. My new career likely insulated me from difficulties other veterans suffered on their return to civilian life. I feel that I returned from combat relatively unscathed. Others close to me might feel differently. But returning to the intensity of the flying environment of that period provided a way to channel the heightened awareness that I'd come to consider as normal. Combat, particularly the kind of specialized conflict at the center of my war experience, prepared me to anticipate the unexpected. In a way, you could say that I never left the war. Those closest to me will tell you I've remained a light sleeper all of my life and that I still scan a crowd looking for those intent on trouble. The situational awareness that helped me survive Vietnam translated well to later responsibilities of flying in an age of mile-high violence. Of course, much of my Vietnam experience was in development of the Kit Carson Scout Program as I've chronicled, so I was used to working with those who'd trained as insurgents mounting guerrilla warfare. The Vietnam War reshaped American thinking in terms of warfare. We can now look back and see America's involvement in Vietnam as our collective entrance into a modern era of war that we still face—war entrenched in ideology and administrated in a manner where we often can't identify our enemies and will rarely see them coming.

The threats my fellow pilots and I encountered in commercial airspace were real. When you pilot a passenger aircraft, you quickly realize that a plane presents a unique environment. Not only is the interior a sealed, contained space (it's not as though emergency assistance is a 911 call away), it's a vehicle that, in the wrong hands, could be turned into a deadly weapon. Once that cabin door closes and the aircraft pushes back from the gate, a pilot has rapid decisions to make with a willingness to accept responsibility for those decisions— including ones with life and death consequences. Up in the sky, pilots are insulated from resources that could resolve most situations that might arise, whether a hijacking attempt, a medical emergency, or an equipment problem. When skies turn menacing, you're all alone.

In many regards, flying in the late 1960s and early '70s bore no resemblance to air travel today. This was true on many fronts, but most notably so in terms of security. When I started my career there was virtually no passenger screening. If a would-be hijacker chose to carry a weapon onto a plane, he could strap guns to every limb and no one would be the wiser unless he were stopped by a suspicious employee who happened to be in the right place at the right time. This was eons before the Transportation Security Administration (TSA), before the use of metal detectors (let alone millimeter wave scanners), and decades before only ticketed passengers passed through security. In those days, most tickets were purchased through a travel agent, and a great deal were sold directly at the airline ticket counter minutes prior to a flight's departure. Families could see their loved ones off at the gate and hijackers could board at will, their only deterrent being their own nerves. If you already had your ticket, you could literally walk from the parking lot to your plane without interacting with a single person until you met one of your stewardesses (as flight attendants were known then—another element of change).

New procedures were implemented as the number of hijacked flights rose, but the airlines remained skeptical about almost all changes to the status quo, fearful that any implemented security measures would make people reluctant to fly. Essentially, big air carriers believed the public's reluctance to fly would be worsened by long wait lines more than the remote possibility of a hijacking. It was still several years before major airlines began to screen carry-on luggage, let alone screen passengers. At the height of the hijacking crisis, the feds instituted observational screening processes primarily undertaken by ticketing agents. Really, they amounted to no more than giving additional attention to those who looked "suspicious", which typically meant someone who either seemed particularly nervous or nearly anyone who looked different from a mostly homogenous flying public. While simplistic, it might've been good policy if the training had been better and if airlines had actually become invested in applying it.

Those things largely didn't happen. It was the rare ticket or gate agent who actively observed people they encountered. By contrast, I'd been highly trained in spotting those who were trying to hide or to blend in for nefarious purposes. My survival in Vietnam depended on being able to do so with accuracy. From the outset of my career, I made it a habit to evaluate those gathered at the gate area and those boarding my plane. I greeted passengers at the doorway to my aircraft as much to assess risk as to provide good customer service. My interest—and my ability—was in identifying intent. If someone behaved oddly, seemed particularly nervous or fidgety, distanced themselves from other passengers, carried a suspicious package or sported a briefcase while not in a businessman's attire, it triggered my radar for trouble and I'd make a point to strike up conversation. Even a casual exchange could likely inform me if I should engage more, alert the attendants to monitor that passenger, or dismiss the person as harmless. Had all flight crews been trained to participate in similar observations and interactions, we could probably have saved a whole lot of heartache, unbelievable stress, money, and, ultimately, lives.

Instead, though pilots held a kind of allure, depicted in the popular media as living glamorous lives, we really weren't provided the tools we needed to protect our planes or our passengers. I believed then and I believe now that pilots need the tools, the training, and the tactical knowledge to take on the threats and emergencies that might occur on a plane. We were quite well trained as pilots and our interests were well represented by our union, the Air Line Pilots Association (ALPA), but we operated in an environment that was nearly entirely focused on safety and not on security. Naturally safety was always of critical importance, but the simple truth was that the world had changed and the industry was slow to change with it. In my experience, pilots and those who represented them were early to the party when it came to recognizing a changing security environment. Federal officials were late comers and some of the airline owners arrived "long after the booze was gone and the music had stopped".

Ironically, among the greatest forces in accomplishing worldwide change—including new applications of threatened or realized violence—was the surge of transcontinental flights. With the increase of worldwide air travel, the globe shrunk. Problems that had once been localized or regionalized could, like deadly, human-carried viruses, spread rapidly and unexpectedly. People could move from one side of the world to another in a matter of hours. Foreign enemies that were once viewed as nearly mythical because they were located so far away began to seem closer. These adversaries were not only informed about US politics through the worldwide presence of American movies, television, music, and news, but that same media fueled their own grievances. Those who wished us harm could now take their political activism to the doorstep of America simply by boarding a plane. For years that meant attempting political leverage by taking hostages and demanding transport, or by seizing a plane in order to claim a ransom. Sticking it to the highly visible airline industry was an overt statement against capitalism. Eventually, airplanes began to represent both symbolic and actual weapons capable of killing thousands and demanding the attention of the world. Airplanes are, by their nature and their history, dramatic objects.

Having worked in the industry from its burgeoning era through the turn of a new century, I'd argue that hijackings in the 1960s and '70s certainly met the definition of terrorism as we define it today. Those past attacks may not have been as lethal as the ones we witnessed on September 11, 2001, but they were motivated by a similar psychology and they preyed upon the same vulnerabilities. And it's not as if September 11th was the first shot fired in a terrorist war. Long before 9/11 we'd experienced the Iranian hostage crisis, the Marine barracks bombing in Beirut, the Pan Am 103 explosion over Lockerbie, Scotland, and the first World Trade Center attack in 1993. Then came the attacks on the Khobar Towers military complex in Saudi Arabia, the bombing of US embassies in Kenya and Tanzania, and the suicide attack on the USS Cole in Yemen. Muslim terrorists had long targeted America, and they were savvy enough to understand both the symbolism of weaponizing an airliner and the enormous impact such tactics would have on the US economy and on American psyches.

Training with FBI SWAT teams in counterterrorism and firearms from 1974 through '76, I'd built numerous contacts in law enforcement and I'd learned about airline security matters in a way none of my peers had. I continued to develop expertise in security techniques and theories, including courses on explosives. I then spent eleven years as a counterterrorism agent working with the FBI responding to active hijackings. As I've shared, this work meant engaging hijackers directly, usually after sneaking onto a compromised plane in the guise of ground personnel or by reporting in as relief pilot during the plane's refueling. In these instances I was always either armed, or if the hijacker demanded a plane change, I'd hidden weapons on board the new aircraft. Often these assignments ended without violence, but I was always prepared to use my skills as a shooter should I have to do so.

Working with the FBI provided me with the expertise necessary for investigating hijacking scenes around the world. Such investigations were important tools in learning more about the motivations, strategies, and techniques of hijackers. During my career, I've interviewed numerous hijackers as well as pilots who were their victims. I also completed the Bureau of Criminal Apprehension School in Minnesota, and I took a number of graduate courses in political science and media technology which deepened my understanding of those with intent to hurt others. Those studies opened my mind to a world whose borders were shrinking with the omnipresence of media and expanding technology. I could foresee that terrorists would seize on such media saturation as a way to broadcast their agendas.

I approached some of the work assigned by the FBI from an entirely tactical perspective, studying ways to terminate a hijacking incident as either an immediate negotiator or as a combatant. But I also studied hijacking occurrences with an eye on developing preventative measures. In my way of thinking, an ounce of prevention really is worth a pound of cure. At the time, theories on prevention took nearly every form imaginable, from psychological studies of apprehended hijackers to the development of nonlethal defense weapons that could stop them in the act. It was also an era that spawned numerous prototype devices to keep assailants from reaching the cockpit, though airlines found a lot of such measures to be unnecessary—if not nonsense. I suspect some simply didn't want to spend the money to retrofit planes or introduce new security protocols.

After eleven years of direct engagement with criminals, an overloaded flight schedule, frequent training with the FBI and stress from the psychological demands of a job that might call upon me to take another life, I was ready—if a bit reluctant—to step down. But stopping this "extracurricular" work did not alleviate my concerns about airline security; nor did it stop me from expanding my education about new security measures and new threats.

By the early 1980s, the avalanche of hijackings suffered by airlines during the previous two decades had slowed. The skies had cleared. But I still thought that we, as an industry, were woefully behind in the security measures we applied. Given the intimacy I'd shared with some of the real dregs of humanity—as a counterterrorism specialist, as a warrior, and as a sheriff's deputy—I feared that we would encounter new threats, including those that raised the stakes profoundly. I'm not proud to be right, but while I could not have known specifics of the attack our country would suffer on 9/11, I'd predicted that type of assault for at least two decades. I wasn't omnipotent. I couldn't foresee what new form terrorism might take or who might conduct it, but I knew that our enemies were no longer oceans away.

I was in a minority, but I wasn't alone. I'd been in regular contact with friends throughout law enforcement and with specialists in the field of counterterrorism. We were bonded by shared interests, similar skill sets, and a passion to protect the public. I was well aware of those, particularly among the FBI and various national security agencies, who were aggressively pursuing leads on what was feared to be a group of jihadists living in America. Because I believed that these concerns of elevated risk would be realized, I openly advocated, mostly among my peers, for new approaches to passenger screening and other advanced security measures.

One of the ironies of flying in those days was our willingness to strap hundreds of people into a steel tube full of fuel, then lock the doors without taking meaningful action toward knowing who those people were or what their intentions might be. Of course, 99.99% of them just want to reach their destination safely and on time, but what were we doing to ferret out that tiny fraction who were intent on harm? What were we doing to provide flight personnel with tools to deal with drunks, selfish agitators, or the mentally unstable onboard their aircraft? The same policies that might prevent a terrorist attack could be used to help flight crews manage threatening passenger behavior.

Encouraged by many of my peers and wanting to draw upon my experience as a commercial pilot, I sought new ways to help the industry I loved to protect those for whom it was responsible. The reputation I'd built at Northwest helped greatly as I considered positions within the Airline Pilots Association (ALPA). People knew me, and for whatever reason they liked me. Nearly all knew of my military background, several knew of my law enforcement expertise, and anyone who knew me recognized my patriotism. I'd like to think that some of them believed I had good ideas.

Early in my career, Northwest management tried to recruit me as a salaried management pilot. I rejected their offer because I didn't want to cross a picket line. This was a strong sentiment in me, probably due to my working-class roots and growing up in a state with a strong union presence. Instead, I worked to stop scab operations. That got my feet wet with the union and introduced me to some of the good people who were working hard to protect pilots' interests. From there I became security coordinator for the local union, a job I held until my retirement. In turn, that experience helped me land a seat on ALPA's Master Executive Council as the Northwest Airlines representative. After years of navigating a political landscape of corporate and government representatives as an advocate for pilots' security needs, I continued to work my way up through the union hierarchy. Eventually I became the chairman of ALPA's Security Committee, a position I was proud to hold for eleven years including those immediately following the 9/11 attacks. Throughout that time I remained actively involved in studying hijackings and other security threats around the world, traveling frequently to Africa, Europe, and Asia to meet with counterterrorism experts as well as pilots who'd been attacked.

In the end, I'd served as an ALPA volunteer for forty-one years, much longer that the thirty-three years I flew for Northwest. Growing up in the woods of Pennsylvania, I could never have imagined that one day I'd meet with members of Congress, share my opinions on Capitol Hill, testify before congressional committees, and see my mug in newspaper articles and on television.

How proud my parents would have been to know that I served our country as a member of the baseline working group of the White House Commission on Aviation Safety and Security overseen by Vice President Gore. I'm sure that they, like others from my youth, would be surprised to know that I chaired the FAA Committee on Aviation Employee Utilization and was a member of the congressionally mandated security subcommittee of FAA's Research, Engineering and

Development Advisory Committee. My role at ALPA also paved my way to become the US representative and vice chairman of the International Federation of Air Line Pilots Security Committee (IFALPA). I even managed to be featured in *Rolling Stone*.

Not bad for a country boy.

All of these roles reflected the expertise on airline security measures that I'd developed over the years, and all furthered my understanding of the motives and methods of those who wanted to breach airline security. As the final Gore Commission report accurately postulated, our industry was one of rapid and constant change. Nowhere was this truer than in the realm of security. We had to keep up with the pace of change in order to stay one step ahead of bad actors. They were innovative and fearless, which meant we had to be ruthless in our pursuit of them and of information pointing toward potential risks in an unpredictable future.

It's hard to overstate how quickly and how overwhelmingly flying has changed in its short history. When the final Gore Commission Report was issued in 1997, just over ninety years had passed since the Wright brothers made history with their twelve-second flight. Only fifty years later, the first commercial jet carried passengers from London to Rome. The first transatlantic commercial flight from New York to London in 1958 lifted off slightly less than ten years before I started my commercial career. But on a sobering note, in less than one hundred years, flying advanced from a heroic effort to keep a plane in the air for 120 feet to the dark act of turning jetliners into fuel-laden weapons. Talk about perspective. Between 1992 and the commissioning of the Gore report in 1996, sixty new airlines had emerged, and in the years between 1980 and 2018, US airline passenger numbers more than tripled.

For the hijacker, seizing control of a plane went from commandeering a news reporter's microphone to taking complete control of a weapon. The hijackers we faced early in my career were interested primarily in gaining notoriety for themselves or highlighting a political cause. After the D.B. Cooper incident, their motives shifted to more of a cash grab. But by the 1990s when I chaired the ALPA Security Committee, hijacking had morphed into a jihad intent on waging war against the West. Aircraft and passengers became their instruments in that war. A lot had changed. Some struggled to fathom that such a change in the tactics of warfare was possible or that suicidal terrorists were training to fly commercial aircraft within our own borders. But information that I was able to access through contacts within federal law enforcement and through my position within ALPA cause me to believe that we came close to unearthing the 9/11 plot before it happened. I remain immensely frustrated by this.

Some things simply hadn't changed. The truth then, and the truth now, is that pilots are more likely to encounter a deranged lunatic, a psychiatric patient off his meds, a really awful drunk, or some enormous asshole wanting to make everyone's flight as miserable as possible than they are to encounter a terrorist on board. Yet I'd been arguing for years that dealing with the ordinary assholes required some of the same security measures needed for those with consciously sinister agendas. The difference is that terrorists are manipulative, taking advantage of sensationalism that draws worldwide attention.

After leading a successful ALPA conference on disruptive passengers in 1997, I initiated an intensive security instruction program for ALPA security volunteers, airline and airport security professionals, pilots, equipment manufacturers, law enforcement officers, and others within the industry. We brought in a number of security experts, including several former and current FBI agents and the ALPA director of engineering and safety, to teach an advanced security curriculum. At ALPA's International Aviation Security Academy (IASA), we taught the most up-to-date countermeasures to protect airplanes and airports from threats ranging from biological weapon attacks, aircraft assaults, chemical weapons attacks, explosives, and missiles. We held sessions on passenger screening and security checkpoints, as well as those focused on transporting deportees and prisoners and how to deal with disruptive passengers.

The academy advanced a "security mosaic" approach that acknowledged the multiple methods and numerous levels of protection necessary for a secure environment. Our method implemented the team concept that we'd developed at ALPA, operating on the principle that everyone within the industry, from baggage handlers and counter agents to flight crews and federal security officials, had a role in preventing tragedies from occurring in the air. Good security is an effective blend of resource management and intelligence. Examining any part of it as a singular issue, without considering the effect that each factor has on the whole, could lead to dangerous and misleading results. To be most effective, security procedures must build as many layers of protection or filters as possible. These defensive features need to be positioned between the threat and the protected asset, a strategy commonly referred to as the onion principle. As layers get closer to the center of the onion—the point of protection—they must become more predictably reliable, less porous, and more effective.

These principles guided all of my thinking and influenced the approaches we took at IASA. I'd engaged in such an approach for most of my career. For example, I'd always made it my habit to meet cleaning crews as they came on board my plane. I'd remind those crews that they were in a unique position to examine the plane and to watch for inappropriate objects, enlisting their help in making the cabin a safe environment. Then I sweetened the deal with sodas or candy bars to thank them for their attention. When it comes to security, the smallest and least glamorous attention to detail can have a great effect.

In the IASA we sweetened the deal in other ways, such as offering tours of FAA's security research and development laboratory and presenting a live demonstration of federal air marshals' marksmanship and anti-hijacking capabilities.

I continued to organize and lead the academy for several years. It was a way for me to combat my growing fear of an escalating threat, and it was a means to prepare for the kinds of attacks addressed by the intelligence community at conferences and in private conversations. A frequent topic was the increasing "chatter" among suspected terrorists detected through ongoing surveillance. Worrisome incidents such as that only confirmed the relevance of our curriculum at the academy. Keep in mind, all of this was happening before the September 11th attacks.

One incident that caught my attention occurred in March of 2000, eighteen months before 9/11. A deranged passenger forcibly breached the cockpit of an Alaska Airlines flight and attacked the crew with their own crash axe, lacerating the first officer's hand. That event didn't surprise me. More than twenty-five years earlier, I was part of a group of tactical experts that studied this problem under the auspices of the FBI; in conjunction with aviation security representatives we brainstormed ways to combat incidents like that one. We listened to tactical experts and technical gadgeteers. We reached a consensus that the best course of action was to terminate the threat through precision use of firearms, preferably directed by a right-handed shooter seated in the first officer's seat.

We analyzed the pros and cons of other approaches to securing the cockpit, including barrier devices, stun guns, and defensive sprays, foams, and gels. My belief was that any weapon, including the standard cockpit crash axe, could be used against a pilot. Such a tactic is common knowledge among law enforcement, for even trained professionals have had their own weapons turned against them. This possibility is heightened in a cockpit setting for two simple reasons: 1) pilots aren't trained or equipped for spontaneous physical combat, and 2) they're always at a disadvantage in forward-facing seats with their backs to the threat.

While I was open to any number of approaches that might keep an assailant out of the cockpit, I felt we had to be prepared to defend the cockpit should one actually penetrate it. The key was to provide pilots with proper firearm and physical training to eliminate at least one of those risks. I remain a strong proponent of arming pilots who volunteer for the rigorous training and near-constant recertification necessary to be effective. It stands to reason that a trained pilot could defend against an attack in progress. But to me, the largest benefit of arming pilots is the uncertainty it would create in a would-be attacker's mind; a terrorist couldn't know if their targeted cockpit was in command of such a pilot. While such deterrence is the purpose of federal air marshals, an armed, well trained pilot is one more important tool in the war against terrorism.

In the years following 9/11, I spent more time on Capitol Hill than I would have liked, promoting ideas for long-overdue security changes for the airlines. I frequently met with members of Congress and urged them to support security measures that would mitigate the risk of repeating the tragedy we'd suffered. I never imagined myself as a lobbyist, but I saw such great danger in the gaping security holes that 9/11 had so clearly unearthed that I was willing to place myself in uncomfortable surroundings. "Uncomfortable" is a way I'd describe Senator Dianne Feinstein's office; held opposite views from mine on nearly every issue. I've been accused of being a bit of a storyteller and a showman, so Capitol Hill—with its liars and reprobates—wasn't entirely out of my league. I had somewhat of an advantage as the outlier, though; I was the interesting new kid on the block rather than the predictable insider wandering around with my palm up and my zipper down. I was a straight shooter and I had confidence.

To resonate with members of Congress, I needed them to view airline security in a concrete and personal way. I appealed to senators and representatives as parents and grandparents. I asked them to imagine what tools they'd want to provide a pilot if one of their loved ones was on board a plane with an armed extremist. I needed them to visualize faces of loved ones if I was to get them to understand the gravity of the risks. The wounds of September 11th were fresh, and those members of Congress traveled with tremendous frequency. Most, though certainly not all, came around to seeing the advantage of the Federal Flight Deck Officer Program (simply referred to as FFDO) which deputized pilots and crew members. Facts began to prevail over sensationalist arguments against the presence of a weapon in trained hands. Many saw as I did that perhaps the greatest strength of the program was the deterrent it provided. The events of September 11th— particularly what transpired on United Airlines Flight 93 when brave passengers thwarted the hijackers' attempts to redirect the flight into the US Capitol—demonstrated that terrorists will target an environment where victims have no real tools with which to fight back. We shouldn't be surprised that since 9/11 Islamic terrorists have attacked "softer" targets, massacring hundreds at the Beslan school in Russia, bombing a commuter train in Madrid, and launching concerted attacks in Paris. Imagine you are a terrorist. Which plane do you want to target, the one where there might be someone armed and trained as your combatant or the one where you face no opposition?

In the immediate aftermath of 9/11, when it came to protecting commercial passenger and cargo planes, FFDO was just one component of needed security and only part of larger legislative action before Congress. Ultimately, the FFDO program became part of the Homeland Security Act passed by the Senate in November of 2002. I'd become known in Washington circles and by media outlets as its vocal advocate. Yet I didn't stop there. I also advocated the design needs of a hardened cockpit door, another critical measure that was subsequently adopted through federal legislation. While I believe that secure cockpit doors are critical to the security of the flight deck, terrorists have taught us that their tactics are innovative and unpredictable and that we should expect them to create measures to breach the cockpit. Keep in mind, even the most effective cockpit doors must be opened to allow pilots to use the bathroom and to attend additional duties required by flight crews.

None of these changes to security measures happened overnight. The creation of the Department of Homeland Security and the passage of the Homeland Security Act (HSA) didn't guarantee rapid enforcement, and, particularly in the case of FFDO, some of its provisions were unpopular. It seemed that many at Homeland Security were dragging their feet. And some of those who ran the newly created TSA didn't believe in it. ALPA helped provide the vision for many aspects of the HSA, and it had been critical to the bill's passage. But passing the bill and implementing its directives were two different animals. I knew that if we were going to be successful in getting measures in place that might prevent a repeat of 9/11—or something even worse—we still had a lot of work to do.

For one thing, I knew that FFDO would have little credibility if we didn't have an experienced and trusted law enforcement official representing ALPA concerns. Jerry Wright, Manager for Security and Human Performance at ALPA, saw the wisdom in my desire to bring someone with law enforcement credentials on board, and he helped me persuade other senior ALPA officials to make a new hire. My longtime friend Howard "Butch" Luker, recently retired from the FBI, was the first to fill the position. Butch had served on an FBI counterterrorism task force for 9/11. He'd been three days from retirement when the terrorists hit. He delayed his retirement to aid the investigation. He brought significant expertise to the investigation, having long served as the FBI airport liaison for the Washington, DC area. Butch and I had worked together on the International Aviation

Security Academy and developed air protection training for the Saudi Arabian security forces. As it turned out, Butch was more a man of action who preferred the excitement of investigation over lobbying and writing position papers, so he eventually stepped aside.

His position was filled by someone I'd heard about but never met, a guy who'd spent twenty-eight years in the Arlington Police Department, mostly as a special investigator. Upon retirement he became the asset protection manager for US Airways. Jim Andresakes spent years working on secret service task forces and he rapidly learned the terrain of airline security. He had a great reputation and I was eager to meet him. As he tells it, I had something of a reputation as well.

Jim provided the law enforcement credibility that I knew we needed. Together we set about building the arguments that would sway both politicians and, more importantly, bureaucrats. We faced opposition from the newly created Homeland Security Department, for not only were many of the decision makers still mired in security standards of the past, but all were wary of the magnitude of change required to implement new protocols. TSA was a fledgling organization that had a tall hill to climb just to hire and train new personnel. Added to that daunting task was the brainstorming of necessary requirements for threat screening, developing known-traveler protocols, and introducing crew member procedures that would include armed pilots. We became close; those who worked with us began to refer to us as Batman and Robin.

As we began lobbying Congress and consulting with working groups in numerous government agencies, I found myself in the unfamiliar territory of the public eye; I was invited to appear on several popular television and radio shows including *Good Morning America, 20-20, Inside Edition,* and *America's Most Wanted.* I guess I got my fifteen minutes of fame after all. As my youngest daughter Megan tells it, on a morning after 9/11 her college roommate shouted a question to her while she was getting ready for the day: "What's your dad's name?"

When Megan replied, her roommate said, "Well, you might want to see this. He's being interviewed by Katie Couric on *The Today Show*." Megan says that was the first time she fully realized that her dad was "sort of a big deal."

Frankly, I had a lot of fun with the press coverage, even if I was more surprised than anyone to find myself on television. I put on my best Armani suit and reveled in my newfound celebrity. Requests from the media poured in. I scrambled to keep up with demands from newspapers, magazines, radio, and television shows. On the serious side, despite good-natured jokes about my notoriety by friends and former co-workers, I recognized how important it was to get our arguments out to the public. We needed public pressure to move politicians to action that was sound and based on the best available security practices. If left to their own devices, uninformed politicians were likely to vote for illogical, trendy, or half-assed measures. They understood the seriousness of 9/11, but they lacked sufficient knowledge of the airline industry to think meaningfully about approaches to prevent future attacks.

It wasn't a time for pussyfooting around. If public appearances gave me the chance to engage with those taking lethargic approaches to security, so much the better. I was always up for a good fight. Besides, the FFDO program was particularly dear to my heart, not only because I thought it could prove a highly effective deterrent to threats, but, I suppose, because of my own long history of flying while armed. I'd been involved directly in many difficult situations where I came face to face with individuals who threatened to do harm. Keep in mind that for a forty-year period, from 1961 until July of 2001, pilots were permitted to be armed with the consent of their airline due to an amendment of federal aviation regulations. Our proposal for establishing the FFDO program was actually a return to and an expansion of long-standing policy. For the FFDO to be effective, advocates needed not only buy-in from Congress (as we had back in

1961) along with several federal agencies, but we also needed to develop a highly specialized, rigorous training curriculum. All of the ALPA proposals committed to the following principles:

- The program would be voluntary;
- Participants would be selected for training only after meeting strict, federal qualification standards;
- Participants would undergo extensive training conducted by a federal law enforcement agency and all training would be specific to protecting the flight deck;
- Those completing training would be deputized as federal officers and their jurisdiction would be limited to the flight deck.

My strategy was to humanize the problem as I lobbied politicians on behalf of FFDO, but I also laid out the specific nature of what the program required. First, the training had to be standardized, providing FFDOs with the best tools and the most current tactical knowledge available to meet the challenges they might face. Second, the curriculum had to be adaptable to meet changing needs and conditions. We needed training updates that were easily deployable and consistently provided. I also felt that the training process had to provide the FFDOs with a sense of institutional pride and belonging. I think this is important in any law enforcement organization. It was critical that FFDOs understood they were deputized federal law enforcement officers, trained and supported by the federal government to protect the aviation component of the nation's critical infrastructure. This was no political grandstand gesture. The FFDO program was a critical component within a larger security mosaic.

Working with other experts, I wrote the requirements for FFDO, outlining the rigorous nature of the training required of these volunteer participants, the recertification requirements, and the protocols regarding pilot screening, weapon transport, and other practical matters needed to make the program work. Our approaches to the program and its pilot training drew heavily from FBI training that a select few and I had received twenty-five years earlier in Operation Switch; they were updated as time and the nature of threats changed. Many of the protocols paralleled those already developed for the Federal Air Marshal Service (FAMS), which integrates plain-clothed, armed federal law enforcement officers among passengers. FAMS officers rank as the most highly proficient marksmen among all federal law enforcement agencies. FFDOs undergo very similar tactical training as FAMS officers due to the unique, high-risk setting of a passenger jetliner.

Despite all the work I invested in getting the FFDO program implemented, I don't view it as the single most important mechanism we can use in threat prevention. As was the case over the course of my career, I emphasized that the most effective security measures involved prevention and protection techniques, centering on a methodical threat vulnerability assessment. Providing security to an airplane meant protecting the cockpit, making it difficult to access. This required training pilots and other crew members in intrusion situation response regardless of whether any of the crew would be armed. It also meant developing the pilots' ability to discern resources among their passengers (for example, the presence of law enforcement personnel, military servicemen and women, and trained medical professionals), including knowing where those resources were seated. Most importantly, we'd need to create risk assessment training so that airline employees could prevent potential threats from ever reaching the jetway. This last element is ultimately the most important. Threat vulnerability assessment is the surest way to protect people when they fly. When done right, it keeps those intent on doing harm from ever having access to a plane. That's key.

It saddens me to say so, but today's approach to security screening continues to assume that anyone who successfully clears the screening checkpoint before entering the "sterile area" is no longer a viable threat. Keep in mind that the only illegal threat item the 9/11 terrorists took on board was their *intention* to do what they had carefully planned and were about to execute.

Threat vulnerability assessment is misunderstood by most civilians, in large part because of media sensationalism. In the press, a complex, nuanced assessment of passengers, based on psychology and focused on intentions of potential criminals, gets watered down to one simple word: profiling. The government is equally guilty of such misunderstanding, for they operate out of fear of overstepping in the realm of individual civil liberties and personal privacy. When viewed through this more simplistic lens, threat assessment becomes politically dicey in a hurry and people assume that such profiling is grounded in racism or religious discrimination. This is simply inaccurate.

Used properly, threat vulnerability assessment examines the likelihood of an individual to be a risk. Our interest, of course, is hostile intent. Such assessment is based on the past behavior and current psychological state of those being assessed. Its foundation is the science of predictable behavior. If a person is flagged through such assessment, he or she is then identified for further scrutiny. Such scrutiny can involve immediate additional screening when that person attempts to take a flight, or it can include background assessment; federal law enforcement officials can examine an individual's criminal record, past behavior, any affiliations with known terrorist groups, and previous foreign travel. Such screening isn't at all unreasonable. Ultimately, a typical passenger is appreciative of the vigilance to assure safety. As for that tiny minority subjected to additional screening— well, it's probably based on some pretty revealing flags. If someone frequents places that are known to harbor terrorist training camps, that person is going to face greater scrutiny no matter the color of his skin or where he worships his god. If someone's been treated for mental illness that manifests in violent behavior, we're going to take a closer look at her. If a person is clearly agitated while waiting in the check-in line, he'll get the attention of the agent on duty. If a Passenger Name Record (PNR) reveals a thirty-year old who, against the grain of common expectation, doesn't have ten years of financial history, it raises a flag of concern. The same is true if one's credit card has been used within the last six months in a country identified by the State Department as having an offending threat-status.

It's intriguing to look back on my life through a post 9/11 lens. When I examine the work I did developing threat assessment profiles, I realize the core skill set that best equipped me for it started in the Pennsylvania woods with my father. What dad taught me by closely observing the woods—looking for little details that could reveal something others would miss, a bent branch, a tuft of hair, the topography of land that would make for the easiest passage—he then extended as lessons for studying people. It's all about trying to read details and studying behavior, looking for what is out of place. For me, the thought processes that allow me to quickly take the measure of a person originated with the skills that made me a good hunter.

As I reflect on this connection, I'm reminded of a hunting trip with my son Judd. Judd's mother and I had been divorced many years by then and Judd and I saw each other only on the occasional weekend or on special trips. When he was a teenager, I flew Judd to Montana to go hunting—his first time hunting elk. We were high up and it was bitter cold, so cold that Judd remembers how at night in the camper I had mounted on my pickup, we wore every layer of clothes we had and stocking caps. When we brushed our teeth, using a miniature paper cup for water to wet our toothbrush, the water would form a thin layer of ice between dips. We were stalking elk and came across moose tracks. We didn't have a moose permit, so we couldn't hunt it, but I thought it might be a rare opportunity to show Judd a moose in the wild. So, I said, "Let's follow these tracks. And I'll bet you anything, this moose is going to know that we're here and it's going to circle around so it can find out what's following it." We followed the tracks for a while until we came up high on a hillside where we could see down below to where we had parked the truck. I told Judd, "Now you watch, we're going to sit here for ten minutes and then that moose is going to come right up out of that clearing and it's going to go right past our truck." Sure enough, a few minutes later here came the moose, exactly as I'd described. If I'd had a license, I could have shot it and have it land five feet from the truck's tailgate. Judd was amazed. He thought I had superhuman abilities. The reality was, I'd simply read the terrain, the weather, the snow, and I thought like a moose.

What I had done with the moose really was what we were asking of threat vulnerability assessment. It's about training yourself to think like the kind of people you are trying prevent from doing harm. In military and police communities we refer to this as situational awareness. The thinking that made me ask a hijacker in Chicago if he wanted a blanket isn't that different. When I was asked to assist with developing risk assessment tools, I was not only drawing on a childhood in the Pennsylvania woods, I was returning to the high stakes observation that kept me alive in Vietnam.

It's a unique skill set. A lot of it can be taught, but there are a few of us who have an ability to assess intent in our DNA. Because I did, I was invited to participate in the development of war games that tried to anticipate terrorist behavior and strategies. Some of the most rewarding intellectual work I've done in my life was assisting Tom Austin, the Lead Threat Analyst for Global Supply Chain Security and Business Continuity, and the Lead System Architect for Chemical, Biological, Radiological, Nuclear, Explosives (CBRNE) Security Countermeasures Programs at the Boeing Company, in these endeavors. While the work we were doing was entire novel and deadly serious, frankly, I found it tremendous fun.

While proper assessment is both an art and a sophisticated science, much of it is rooted in common sense. The simple reality is that when you're looking for snakes, you've got to turn over a few rocks. The current process of passenger assessment is based on an assumption that everyone is a threat, from the ninety-year-old wheelchair-bound grandmother to a group of school children. Rather than using clear parameters to assess individual threats, we subject every passenger to one intrusive process, creating the long security lines and reactive measures that our traveling public hates.

Equally important in a security environment: By using the same screening methods for everyone, we tip our hand for those we *should* be worried about. And those responsible for security waste valuable time picking the fly shit out of the pepper. If you can keep the flies out of the pepper in the first place, it makes everything else a lot easier. How many shoe bombers have we actually caught by making everyone take off their shoes? The really bad guys get smarter all the time. They change their game. They see where there are no longer vulnerabilities within a security system, but they're constantly looking for new vulnerabilities. On the other hand, security protocols, particularly those emplaced by larger bureaucracies, tend to be reactive rather than proactive; they tend to confuse the means with the end.

I advocate for the following: Reserve invasive measures and more advanced checks for those who can run those assessments effectively. Then layer that approach with the use of more dogs trained to sniff out chemicals, explosives, weapons, and drugs. Aggressive screening would likely draw criticism, but applying the same security procedures to everyone doesn't stop accusations of profiling anyway.

Keep in mind that today's airport security—TSA, secure passenger areas, restricted access terminals, chemical checks, body scans, etc.—were largely nonexistent before 9/11. Yet I'd been advocating for the equivalent of what is now TSA PreCheck and the CLEAR program decades ago, insisting that most passengers are not any sort of threat at all. For most, one comprehensive screening process would be sufficient rather than subjecting them to ineffective checks each time they fly. I supported this view with my knowledge of emerging technology such as biometric identification through eye scans, fingerprints, and the like. I used to demonstrate my point by bringing a large box of ping-pong balls into meetings. I'd mix a handful of pink and purple balls in among a huge number of white ones. When I would dump the box onto a conference table, people got my point.

We need security apparatus in place just as we need highly trained flight crews, but I remain convinced that we can create a safe environment more efficiently than we do and with less intrusion on people's lives. Programs like TSA PreCheck allow minimally invasive background checks and assign a known-traveler number to those approved. This ties into all future flight reservations as evidence of positive background screening.

Even more in keeping with what I'd imagined nearly twenty years ago is the CLEAR program; it uses fingerprints and retinal scans to establish identity, allowing fast, minimal on-site screening which "clears" passengers who've had their security clearance authorized in a manner that can't be replicated. In essence, security personnel know who these passengers are because they've already done the background investigation. There's a simple mathematical reality here: If security enforcement officials can focus nearly all of their energy on that micro-percentage of people who really are more likely to be a threat, they can do their jobs far better. They're no longer looking for a needle in a haystack; they're only examining a manageable bundle of needles.

We used to be up against another bit of math as well. Before the advent of computers, behavioral prediction relied upon the acuity of a few individuals. Now, instead of running a few dozen or a few hundred probabilities, thousands can be run with ease. Today those few individuals—trained behavior prediction experts—can now manage the vast data that modern technologies provide. We've entered an era where, if the government has the will to apply such science intelligently and on a wider scale, we can put such powerful tools to work.

Many of the advanced screening protocols now used by TSA were developed by me and others like me who were heavily invested in airline security. I only wish they were used more widely and robustly. At ALPA, we developed a team concept that combined a number of the measures I've described and aimed to provide awareness training for every employee from the parking lot to the gate check-in counter. Crew members fly all over the world, interface with literally thousands of people daily, and become acutely aware of abnormal and unusual behavior—even the subtleties most likely hidden from the casual, uninitiated observer. The aircraft is their home and they frequently spot things that are overlooked by people who don't "live" there. They must learn to trust their instincts and capture their observations, as must employees throughout the airport and within flight operations. Such a "sixth sense" detection/protection program had been grossly overlooked throughout the 20th century and remains vastly underdeveloped in the 21st. Applying it consistently is a starting point. Beyond that, current expertise along with new technology can enhance such basic detection. Sophisticated threat vulnerability assessment algorithms and psychological databases already exist within government agencies and among research entities of the airline industry. I only hope that we can change the political climate in a way that allows us to put some of them to use. Doing so would make air travel exponentially safer.

Nothing about airline security is simple. Consider, for example, all of the different vectors through which a threat can enter any commercial aircraft: cargo, mail, fuel, food, and supplies, as well as passengers, carry-on baggage, checked baggage, and all personnel with direct aircraft access. Add to these the threat potential from those vectors with non-direct access: surface to air missiles, lasers, drones, other aircraft. Now consider the complexities of trying to sustain a flow of passengers with minimal disruption in an environment where the sheer volume is mind boggling. For example, in 2018 over a hundred million passengers passed through the Atlanta Hartsfield International Airport alone. Factor in all of the entities with high stakes involvement in managing air traffic and risk management: commercial passenger airlines, commercial cargo air transport companies, airports, airplane manufacturers, organizations representing flight personnel like ALPA and the Association of Flight Attendants (AFA) along with its union the Communication Workers of America (CWA), government agencies including TSA, the Department of Homeland Security, FAA, the FBI, and the Department of Transportation. Whew!

Meanwhile, by contrast, even the most organized terrorist groups are small, nimble, and secretive. Even more difficult to combat is the nutcase lone wolf—motivated by alignment with terrorist groups or political causes, suffering delusions of self-grandeur, or driven to violence by mental illness. Identifying such threats is hard enough; creating a coordinated response that addresses all threat vectors and communicates across densely layered bureaucracies is extraordinarily demanding.

That high-risk environment was my office for thirty-three years. Who better to develop measures for securing an airplane than the people whose responsibility it was to land it safely at the end of every flight? This concept was a major factor in the ALPA Security Committee's legitimacy. Policy makers in the aviation community and federal law enforcement saw us as vital partners. Not only were we the most consistent voice for the flying public's interests, we possessed an expertise that even the most experienced FBI agents or FAA authorities lacked. They didn't have their butts strapped in the pilot seat and they didn't have the fate of five-hundred passengers at their fingertips while they controlled a plane with 633,000 pounds of thrust. In my years as chairman of the ALPA Security Committee, I'd worked many long nights with a phone at my ear and a pee bottle by my side when dialed in to FAA's crisis command post during an active situation with an aircraft. Sometimes my assistance was based upon my own years in dealing with similar situations. Sometimes I merely applied mundane, seat-of-the-pants knowledge that I'd gained from decades in the cockpit; I knew its layout without having to actually see it. I knew a plane's quirks, its capacity, and the logistics of its flight. I appreciated the willingness of those dedicated to securing the skies to allow a pilot a seat at the security table. And I'm proud to have participated in reducing the chance of a future tragedy. The most important work of my career culminated in my selection to receive the ALPA David Behncke Lifetime Achievement Award, the highest honor ALPA can bestow upon a member of the organization. I'm humbled to have been the third person in the organization's history to receive this honor.

I knew I had a direct hand in saving some lives in Vietnam and making my little corner of that country incrementally safer; but my career in aviation security made me feel that I'd contributed to something bigger. Repercussions of security policy decisions directly impact millions of lives, and I'm proud to have contributed what I did. I entered adulthood fast and furiously when I set foot in Vietnam. When I departed from ALPA, I continued to train and consult for many more years, but I'd reached the other bookend in my life. There's an inescapable irony of those two experiences and the decades between them. I'd been tracked for advancement in Vietnam and again by Donald Nyrop at Northwestern because of my ability to kill—yet I focused the majority of my professional life on saving lives. I've found life to be full of such ironies. They're just two sides of the same coin.

One Shot at a Time

"Whatever good things we build end up
building us."
—Jim Rohn

I've had a lot of good in my life. Good people. Good mentors. Good wives. Good children. Good friends. Good opportunities. Lots and lots of good opportunities. I'd like to think I've done some good for others as well. I tried to do so, even if it's easy to admit that I'm full of flaws and I probably haven't done enough. It's been a fun ride, though. My daughter Sarah likes to tell me she thinks I've lived enough for several lives.

At my heart I'm little more than a street fighter, or whatever you'd call the equivalent of a street fighter who grew up in the woods. I'm a scrapper. I don't often find the easiest route forward, but I always find my way. I've had a "get 'er done" attitude long before comedians and country music made the phrase popular. And I've always believed that you get out what you put in. As a result, I threw myself into everything I attempted throughout my life. That attitude probably defines me best. I like action. I've taken things as they've come—one shot at a time.

Another trait that defines me is that I've never taken crap off of anyone. I've always been an open book, so I have no tolerance for those who like to play games. I state what's on my mind and I expect the same from others.

And a third quality central to my personality is that I'm curious. I like to know how things work. I pay attention. I try to see and to think in ways that others don't.

Those traits all served me really well in the Marine Corps as they did throughout my flying years and during my work as a security specialist. They didn't always serve me as well as a husband or father. I guess it would be fair to say that it took me a long time to grow up in a lot of ways—certainly in how I treated the women in my life. For whatever reason I seemed to always have good bait, and that meant I had a lot of girlfriends ... even during my first two marriages. The airline industry in the '60s and '70s could be a bit of a Peyton Place, and there was no shortage of pretty flight attendants or nights away from home. It wasn't a fair thing to the women in my life or to my children, but I was guilty of taking advantage of such circumstances. I don't make such admissions out of any sort of boasting. I may be guilty of telling fish stories but I like to traffic in facts. I don't wish to hurt anyone by revealing the truths of my past, but I'm not going to hide behind it either. Like I said, I believe in being honest and I like to hear honesty from those around me.

Of course, the actions we take and the decisions we make have consequences. While I most certainly loved my first wife, Syble, I was a young, tempestuous man when I met her. I was enthralled with her beauty. She was from Brewton, Alabama, and I flew a lot of training missions into the airfield there, which was part of the larger Naval Air Station Pensacola. I first met her at a party. Our initial romance could have come straight out of *An Officer and a Gentleman* (substitute a Marine aviator for a Navy one). Local girl falls in love with an officer. As a teenager she'd been crowned the Alabama Poultry Queen, and poultry is no small thing in the state of Alabama so I don't exaggerate her beauty or her infectious personality. All these decades later, I jokingly refer to her as the Chicken Queen. We were young and foolish and probably didn't start out with much of a grown-up concept of love. The nature of our love could be pretty fierce, as could our fights.

I'd returned home from Vietnam in 1967 focused on getting on with my life, starting a career, and looking fully forward, something

I've done ever since. As I've detailed, I'd not only seen a lot of death during my thirteen months there, I'd worked within sectors of clandestine intelligence operations that left me uncertain about how much of the world operated. I'd had all the adrenaline rushes one body can probably take. I suppose I carried my demons from the war, though I tried not to think about them. No good could come from dwelling on my experiences. Demons have a way of hanging around in the shadows. They remain dangerous whether we see them or not.

The other truth was that a big part of me still wanted to be in Vietnam. I believed in the work I was doing there. The Kit Carson Scout Program was still in its infancy, and, as I've admitted elsewhere, I'd never felt as alive as I had in Vietnam. I loved that adrenaline. Syble wanted nothing to do with my going back. At times that was a bone of contention for me. We'd rushed into the marriage and my oldest daughter, Stephanie, was born even before I'd departed for the war. In any case, back in the civilian world, I threw myself into the dream I'd had since I was a teenager—one that involved airplanes.

The pilot corps of the airline industry was built largely of men who'd exited the military, so despite the fact that much of our country treated Vietnam veterans like shit stuck to the bottom of their shoes, I entered a place where I was among a lot of men with whom I could relate. I was able to trade one uniform for another. There's something transformative about putting on a uniform when you go to work each day. I liked the sense of responsibility, I liked the notoriety that surrounded me, and it was easy to focus on finding the fastest track to the captain's seat. That meant that most of the work rearing our little family fell on Syble. She was a trooper, moving out of the South for the first time in her life, away from her extended family and into the cold of Minnesota where Northwest was based. I was so focused on moving ahead that I probably didn't do enough to take her feelings or her needs into full account and I was so tired when I was around that I probably wasn't worth much.

Like most of life, marriage could be rocky at times and blissful at others. I loved my family, but I didn't have a lot of time for them. In those early years the airline industry was a turbulent place. There was strike after layoff after strike. I became involved with the union and was known as something of a scab buster. Northwest was running an operation with non-union pilots that we were trying to stop. We were trying to maintain the integrity of our pilot group so that it didn't abrogate the credibility of the negotiating process. Once in a while we had a hell of a time controlling our people. It was important to protect our interests and keep the scabs out but equally important not to lose our leverage by overstepping. I seemed to be someone people listened to, so my involvement with the union intensified.

Those union responsibilities led to others, and I began to apply the expertise I'd developed while in Vietnam to address the ever-increasing needs of security. ALPA was known and respected for the careful and thorough work it had been doing on airline safety issues for many years, and this ability was invaluable as it began to shift more focus to security. Meanwhile I was putting in my time in the air and taking the routes others thought they were too good for. As I've detailed, flying could be a dangerous activity in the late '60s and much of the '70s—one made worse after the D.B. Cooper incident—and the particular work Mr. Nyrop requested of me added its own element of stress. I was torn in a lot of directions at once. Syble and I made the marriage last for over ten years, but between the distance and the actions we'd both taken our relationship had become a broken thing.

I was away for an important part of Stephanie's first year while I was in Vietnam. I missed out on seeing her learn to walk, along with a lot of other firsts. I wish I could say that pattern changed upon my return, but I'd be lying. I was simply pulled in too many directions at once, something that remained true for nearly my whole career. Because she was the oldest, I'm sure she was aware of the problems between her mother and I more than I would wish for her to know. I have regrets about that and about being away so much. But I'd always taught my kids the old adage: "To whom much is given, much is expected." I tried to live by that. I still believe it with all my heart but it does bring consequences.

The times I did have with my kids are special to me. From the very beginning, Stephanie was sharp and independent. She was tough. She was the sort of kid who hit every benchmark early, from walking and talking to becoming smarter than her dad. She was never the sort to let the grass grow under her feet. Her affinity for the fast track hasn't changed since childhood—she's ascended to senior executive positions with two of the largest and most respected corporations in America. She always challenged herself, earning her way into a demanding private college, St. Olaf. From there she one-upped me and completed a master's degree even while working her first job out of college as a human resources manager at—where else—Northwest Airlines. Truth be told, her academic achievement is more due to her mother than to me, but I hope I can take some credit for her ambition and drive. As a senior executive, she holds levels of responsibility few can imagine, and she never flinches.

Her brother, Judd, came along in 1969. A quieter sort than any of my other children, Judd was contemplative and introspective. Though a child at the time, I'm sure the divorce scarred him in ways I can't fully imagine. I became the kind of father that a divorce in the 1970s created—too often absent, a kind of play thing for him yet a bit of a stranger even when I was present. Because Stephanie was older than her brother, I assume that left her with more feelings of anger than he held. I'm only projecting what I believe to be true, as I cannot speak for my children, but I suspect Judd was more confused by how his life changed and he probably thought he'd done something wrong. As for Stephanie, I would guess there were times she learned to hate me as only women can hate men and then times when I'm sure she longed for her father.

For a while Judd wanted to follow in my footsteps. During college he trained to be a pilot before discovering that he had an eye condition which kept him from qualifying. He did, however, put in his own time at Northwest, in the sort of work where people learn the value of a hard day—handling baggage. Unable to fly professionally, he studied the engineering of flight and graduated with a degree in aeronautical engineering from the University of North Dakota. This was on top of another degree in psychology from Carleton College. Like his sister, Judd rose through the corporate ranks—in his case, he excelled in the world of technology as a software engineer. He's now a vice president of engineering at Infoblox. As with his sister, I'd like to take credit for his brains—I mean, after all, my academic strong suit had always been math and science—but where I saw college as my ticket to Officer Candidate School, Judd has helped develop technology so far advanced from what we considered the epitome of high tech in the Marine Corps fighter cockpit that I can't entirely comprehend it.

I've done my share of setting the example for working hard for success. I'm willing to boast—just a little, at least—as I remember hearing the pride in my son's voice when he called to tell me that he'd come across an article that quoted me in *Rolling Stone*. I'm happy for those kinds of moments.

I didn't always make their lives easy. I'd met a pretty young flight attendant who threw me for a loop. Bev was in her early twenties when we met and still in the beginning years of her career. She was the sort of young woman who thrived as a flight attendant—attractive and smart, funny and caring. In those days the airlines always had a lot more women line up to fill positions than they had jobs available, so you kind of got the cream of the crop. Bev fit that bill. And, apparently, she didn't hold my reputation against me. We married within six months of my divorce being finalized. I've always been the sort of man who follows my instincts and my heart. Sometimes life just happens.

Shortly after Bev and I were married I went on a hunting trip in Montana. I'd grown to love the state and I spent as much time there as I could. At my heart I'm a cowboy, even if I am better with cars than I am with horses. Montana had fueled my imagination since I was a kid. I romanticized the place, associating it with stories I'd read during childhood—myths of the Old West and its cowboy heroes. As an early teen my best friend was Clayton Price; Clayton's father wore a belt buckle embossed with the state name *MONTANA*. I thought it was the neatest belt buckle I'd ever seen. I even loved the sound of the word.

When I flew with Northwest and I saw routes going to Montana, I thought, "Wow—I've got to go there." And so I did. During a hunting trip in the Tobacco Root Mountains, I talked about merits of that state with another pilot friend by the name of Jim Hystad. Jim was a great big bear of a guy and one of my best hunting buddies. We always knew how to have a good time together. Sharing a desire to settle in that "big sky country", we finally concluded: "Well, hell, we're pilots. We can live anywhere we want." So the two of us bought adjacent twenty-acre plots. When I got home I told Bev, "Guess what? I bought twenty acres and a horse in Montana."

Once she was over the shock, Bev started to get behind the idea of living a quieter life and starting a family in the West. Always one to roll with the punches, she joined me as I started building a house on the property in 1978. Manhattan, Montana, a one-horse town if ever there was one, was quite a change from Minneapolis/St. Paul— let alone other cities our routes took us to with such frequency. Moving to Montana felt like coming home. During our first night there we had no electricity and no running water, so we heated water in a coffee pot to wash our faces and used the porta potty in the camper that we'd hauled to the property.

We started by building a garage with a large apartment above. We spent most nights with friends or housesitting other homes during its construction. Once completed, the garage housed my shop and my toys—for decades a must in any place I've called home. The apartment had a living room, kitchen, bathroom, and a large master bedroom with two 4x8-foot closets that eventually became the spaces where our two toddlers slept. (Sarah came along in 1979 and was joined by her sister Megan two years later.) We lived in that above-garage apartment for three years while we built the main house. Our girls said that living there while we built our home always felt like camping. We finally finished the house in 1983 and then moved to Montana full time.

The house took years to build because Bev and I did nearly all the work ourselves on our days off from flying. Most of the time we flew together so we could coordinate our time in Montana. Back in those days, while the frequency of strikes and layoffs could make working in the industry topsy-turvy, the scheduling for air crews was much better than it is today. This allowed us to maximize our productivity during our time off. When the kids were little, Bev could work three days while her parents watched the kids, and then she'd have several days at home with the girls before her shifts started again.

I learned much of what I knew about construction from my dad, and I'd become a licensed plumber and electrician while I was still a teenager. Friends and family would fly in and help us with the house when they could, including my dad and several of Bev's relatives. The only work we hired out was installation of the septic system and the stonework on the outside of the house. I didn't lay the rock but I did haul it all in from the Bridger Range. The stone we used for the hearth was slate that I brought all the way from Pennsylvania, so I've got a little bit of my childhood roots in that house as well.

Not only was our construction time limited by our flying schedules, but the house was no small affair at over 5,000 square feet. We did it right, using custom finishes throughout. I hand built the banister and railings and all of the trim work. If I was flying and Bev was off duty, she'd be hard at work staining trim and cabinets, painting, and finishing other tasks. When we worked together, she was always on the on the other end of the board I was cutting or the sheet of drywall we were hanging.

I took pride in completing work for myself. We put our hearts into that house, and it became the center of our young family. Years after our marriage ended and the house sat empty for far too long, Sarah moved there with her own young family. I'm so happy to see that the house stayed in the family and is now home to a new generation. Visiting her family, I feel as though the house has lived on and that the good memories there are still contained within its walls.

I'd initially gone into commercial aviation to provide stability for my family, yet the reality was that my first two children lived with their mother, not with me. I tried not to repeat the patterns of my first attempt at fatherhood. I committed myself to being far more involved in Sarah and Megan's lives. It helped that I was approaching the age of forty when Sarah was born, for not only was I more aware of the kind of parent I wanted to be, I was far enough into my career that I'd moved up to larger planes, better routes, and bigger money. I mostly flew long-haul routes by then, so much of the time I might fly ten days straight and then have ten days at home. Though I still had my fingers in a lot of pies, I was able to schedule time at home in patterns that allowed me to help Bev with the kids more and gave me more one-on-one time with them. Still, let's face it—a pilot is gone a lot, and I was heavily involved in multiple aspects of the airline industry.

The Montana house proved a great place to raise a family. Jim Hystad never built on his twenty acres, but he granted us full access to it as compensation for taking care of his horses. Essentially we had forty acres to ourselves most of the time. Game was plentiful right on our land, and while Bev, the kids, and I took frequent hunting trips in the surrounding mountains, we shot a good number of deer right there on our property. I passed along the knowledge I gained through hunting, riding, and hiking to my girls, taking them antelope hunting outside Livingston, Montana or having them help skin the deer I killed on our own small acreage outside Manhattan, Montana. For Sarah and Megan, like they had been for me, the woods were both a schoolhouse and a playground. I know they have fond memories of camping trips and trail rides, of screaming around the prairie and farmlands on ATVs and fishing on pristine rivers.

I vowed that our girls would grow up knowing how to handle guns, how to handle themselves, and how to work hard. By the time Sarah was five, I could shoot a deer at the tree line on the edge of our property, whistle to get her attention, and she'd jump into a pair of boots and come out to hold a leg for me while I gutted. I'd throw the deer onto the three-wheeler, lift Sarah onto my lap, and we'd haul it to the garage where she helped me skin. Within a couple of years Megan followed suit. They were never what you'd call squeamish girls.

Sarah is a Montana girl through and through. As natural a shooter as I am, she killed seven big game animals—four antelope and three deer—with eight shots on one her first hunts with me. Not only is she a mighty fine shot, she's better on a horse than I am. I like horses but I love engines, so we used to tear around our property and over forest trails on three-wheelers. Sarah is stable, tender, and comforting in ways that I've never been. We always needed someone with a level head in this family, and she's always provided it. I'm not surprised that she chose a career in education—now as a reading specialist—that allows her to help people. I'm proud of the fact that she's changing the lives of little kids for the better and doing it right there in the little town where she was raised.

I taught Sarah, and her sister too, how to drive by bumping along our horse pastures in an old Jeep. We'd hunt, camp, and hike, and most of all we'd dance in the living room to good country music— George Straight, Randy Travis, Reba McEntire, the Judds—and we always had the radio blasting in the car. Sarah and I share a lot of the same taste in music, and she was always my go-to dance partner when a great song came on the radio. That music must have run right into her sister's bloodstream because, in addition to being a businesswoman and travel expert, Megan is a songwriter, recording artist, and performer. In the vein of all of my kids but maybe more overtly so, she is fearless. Nothing scares Megan. She is probably the most like me of any of my children. Well, not in the musical sense. I'm not sure where that came from. But she definitely inherited my wild side and my independent spirit.

I wanted all my kids to be tough and to stand up for themselves and they've all made me proud in this way. Megan sort of embodies that. When Megan was a freshman in high school, she desperately wanted to be part of the cheerleading squad. She was told that the squad was full but that they anticipated openings in the spring when one of the girls would quit cheer squad to run track. That opened up the prospect that she could work out with them, learn the routines, and travel to away games, but there was also a catch: She'd have to be the mascot. Undaunted, Megan pulled on the smelly, sweaty, threadbare tiger costume. She didn't just endure a role that must have felt humiliating for a fourteen-year-old girl—she owned it. She had the attitude that if she had to be the mascot, she'd be the most entertaining mascot that Manhattan, Montana had ever seen. She hammed it up, played to the crowd, and even brought her lasso to games where she'd rope the opposing team's mascot. One time she pulled this routine on an oblivious opponent and accidentally landed him on the gym floor. My youngest daughter always could throw a mean punch. Still can.

The girls and I have stayed on good terms despite the ending of my marriage to their mother. We separated when Sarah was sixteen and Megan was fourteen. I know it was hard on them, but Bev and I had been pretending the marriage wasn't over for at least a couple of years. Bev and I tried to insulate them from the problems in our marriage, working hard to make the split as positive for the girls as possible and giving them two loving, supportive families where once there was one. Bev and I were able to retain the best parts of our relationship and have since remained good friends.

When Bev and I accepted that our marriage was over in all but the legal sense, my life took another twist. Marsha was a special woman: kind to everyone, with love to give in abundance. She had a personality that was magnetic. Everybody who ever knew her liked her. We'd been work colleagues for years—another flight attendant, she was impressive in the way she went about her job. Passengers loved her. She was a very passionate person, not just about family—she had two sons from a previous marriage and immediately welcomed my kids into her life—but she also cared deeply about issues such as women's rights, motherhood, and patriotism. The right stuff. She made me a better person; there was something about her nature that took the best elements of my personality and amplified them. And maybe some of the less desirable parts of Steve Luckey were tamped down because of her presence in my life.

Sadly, my time with her was cut short. We were a couple for several years before we married in 2000—only to have our honeymoon upended when Marsha learned she'd been diagnosed with ovarian cancer. The next three years were the toughest of our lives. She fought like a trooper, never flinching even as the treatments failed and the disease ravaged her body. She showed bravery like I've never witnessed.

Those years caring for Marsha have left an indelible mark on my life. Never had I felt so lost and so helpless. I'm not a person accustomed to inaction. But cancer doesn't allow you to take charge. Watching Marsha suffer and not being able to take her pain away is the hardest thing I've ever faced in my life. But my life is so much richer for having her in it. Caring for her during her battle with cancer made me a better man.

I have no idea what I've done in my life to be so blessed, but even amid the heartache of losing Marsha another inspiring woman entered my life. I'd actually known Jeannie years before because her first husband, Bill, was a fellow Marine aviator. I'd trained with Bill and had known him for decades. Bev and I were good friends with Jeannie and Bill, even traveling to Hawaii together once.

I hadn't seen Jeannie in years. I was living on a ranch in Pony, Montana and flying in and out of the Bozeman airport. Jeannie and Bill had introduced Bev and me to lots and lots of people around Bozeman during our years in Manhattan, and I'd become good friends with several of the people we met. Among them were Don and Bonnie White. Don and I did a lot together and frequently hunted for elk up near Big Sky. For a number of years Don organized fishing trips to Alaska, and boy, did we haul in some fish.

When Marsha died I talked with Don, who was an attorney, about some of the complications of settling her estate and managing our investments. Don wisely encouraged me to consult with Jeannie, who was a financial advisor and investment management consultant. Jeannie and Bill had divorced a couple of years earlier and she was living in Kalispell, Montana. So, I drove five hours northwest to seek advice from my old friend. If a lot of my life resembles a movie, this particular era definitely fell into the romance category. We were that movie couple who'd survived the plot twists and turns of complicated lives—friends who came together late in the story to realize they were meant for each other. It was like we'd reached a new stage in our lives and were able to see each other in a new light.

Jeannie jokes that she's actually known me a good portion of her life, ages before her husband and I extended our friendship to include our wives. Jeannie remembers meeting me briefly when she was still in high school. Talk about small world. Bill and I had managed to get ourselves in a fight with a bunch of sailors (big surprise) at a party in the Georgetown part of Washington, D.C. I couldn't tell you what caused the fight—seems like fighting, booze, and young Marines aren't exactly an unpredictable mix—but I'm quite confident we came out on the better end. I was probably all of twenty-two or so. How was I to know that the pretty young thing who was interested in my friend would become, some forty years later, my wife?

Finding Jeannie all those decades later when she was emerging from the rubble of a bad marriage and I was reeling from the loss of my wife was a kind of magic. It felt like the universe had dropped an angel into my world. It's hard to describe, but something between us fit like the missing piece of a puzzle. I sometimes wonder if we hadn't been looking for each other all of our lives and just didn't know it. Being with Jeannie felt like the most natural thing in the world. She is one of the rare women in the world who can put up with me, and she's strong enough to stand up to me when I need it (which is pretty frequent).

Case in point, part of our honeymoon was probably not the sort of trip Jeannie would have knowingly signed on for. Like a lot of my stories, this one is of the "I knew a guy who knew a guy" variety. My good friend Cecil Bell, with whom I'd flown at Northwest and who had helped me get the outfitting business going, knew a somewhat famous deep-sea fisherman who lived in Tasmania. The guy had invited us to come down and said he'd take us out lobstering and fishing. He was an Irish guy and was married to a Moroccan Muslim woman. He'd even been knighted by the Queen because he'd saved so many people at sea over the course of his career. I thought, what the hell, a trip to fish new waters with someone who was an expert—not exactly your typical honeymoon, but it could be a good time.

Jeannie is game for just about anything, but despite being a damn good shot and able to wrangle a 4-wheeler, she's more of the "Let's stay at the Four Seasons" kind of gal than "Let's experience the four seasons in a tent. But a tent it was—a ratty one at that. Night found us hunkered down in it, restless sleeping bags that looked like they'd been chewed on by racoons. But the tent might have been a step up from the fishing boat. Jeannie swore she'd find a spot on the rocky beach over stepping foot in the head.

We were camped on a remote shoreline. I wished you could have seen the look on Jeannie's face when, about 2:00 in the morning, we were awoken by the loudest, shrillest animal call I've ever heard in all my years out in the wild. Jeannie's face said, "Why was it I agreed to this trip?" I was more worried if she was second guessing why she'd thought it fit to marry me. I spent the night wishing I had a shotgun to go dispatch whatever it was that had made the sound. In the morning we learned the sounds were calls from Fairy Penguins, which make a grunting racket at night.

Needless to say, Jeannie stayed married to me despite the honeymoon. Our time together has been filled with adventures only cut short by my declining health. We are both curious, passionate people deeply invested in our professions and eager to continue growing. She's smarter than anyone I've ever known—and, like me, she thrives on hard work. She's driven in a way that I've always been. I was impressed with the life she'd built for herself and impressed with her independence. She was deeply involved in her community and owned her own business; I was shocked when she so readily allowed me to be part of it. We made each other better when we were together and immediately set out to make up for lost time, marrying in 2004. Jeannie has been my wife, my best friend, and my business partner all rolled into one.

Marrying Jeannie also brought another set of kids into my life, albeit grown ones. Because Jeannie and Bill and I had been friends for decades, I'd known Jeannie's kids, mostly from a distance, all of their lives. Jeannie and I love each other's kids. In this most recent period of my life, when my health has restricted me to a skilled nursing facility to get the daily support I need to manage my MS, Jeannie's daughter,

Jennifer, is a welcomed and frequent visitor. She's good about bringing me treats and good conversation and she put bird feeders up on my window to bring a little bit of nature back into my life. In some ways, I understand Jennifer's brother, Chris, the best because he was a Marine and a pilot, so we think a lot alike. Chris and his family live in the same town as Jeannie and I, so we get the pleasure of seeing his daughter more often than my other grandchildren. But I'm closest to Bill, probably because we've spent the most time together and we both love to hunt. He's been a tremendous support to me in the last several years, helping me around the house and becoming my legs now that mine no longer work. To have such a large, loving, and high-achieving family is a blessing beyond anything I deserved.

After retiring from Northwest in 2000 and then from the security advisor role with ALPA several years later, I kept my feet in the water by forming a consulting company that I named Jetana International Security. This continued my travels abroad, including my stint teaching in Saudi Arabia that I've described. I also contracted work in Indonesia and elsewhere around the world that, due to confidentiality pledges, I can't detail. From 2007 until 2011 I served as a consultant for Boeing, working on aviation security-related projects and security threat modeling, much of which remains classified.

Though we kept the ranch in Pony and built a house and other structures on the property together, we settled our primary residence in Kalispell where Jeannie ran her investment business. There I sustained my passion for guns and gun sports and began working with local Montana gun manufacturers on firearm design and development. I also continued to gunsmith, something I'd done all my life. Simply keeping up with the gun repair and customization needs of my many friends could have been a full-time job. I guess it's worth repeating that I am blessed to have a lot of good friends as well as a talent to make a marginal firearm perfect.

Jeannie and I embarked on another personal security project we'd started brainstorming early in our marriage. As we watched a world where crime continued to escalate while more and more social norms dissolved, we thought people—especially women—needed a reliable, nonlethal means to protect themselves. Knowing my background, Jeannie encouraged me to think about how such a device might best work. From our many discussions, The Defender was born. Jeannie probably had more good ideas regarding The Defender than I did, and certainly she possessed the business know-how required to get a product out of our imaginations and into the market.

We envisioned a gun-shaped weapon (people have an instinctual reaction to the lethality of anything that looks like a gun) that sported a number of mechanisms that could be used to dissuade a would-be attacker. We designed The Defender so that its platform could easily and quickly accommodate any number of nonlethal features, including a pepper spray cylinder, a high intensity flashlight, a strobe, a noisemaker, and a taser. If none of those worked, we made the whole thing sturdy enough to beat the asshole you were defending yourself against. Each accessory used technologies that were well tested throughout the larger industry. For example, the noise device created a loud, shrill tone so high on the spectrum that people would just about crawl out of their skins to get away from it. Such sound technologies are regularly used by law enforcement during riot or stand-off situations. Items such as pepper spray have been tested for decades, used regularly in smaller personal-protection devices, employed by police in crowd control and barricade breaches, and, in places like Montana, designed to protect against grizzly bears. The beauty of such devices is that—with sprays and tasers effective from at least ten feet and features such as sound devices creating an even larger defense zone—they keep assailants distant from their targets.

We found a wonderful manufacturer for The Defender in Gary Byers, owner of a company called Creative Sales in Columbia Falls,

Montana. Gary had formed a company within Creative Sales called Pro-Defense, which produced a rail-mounted pepper spray system. Working with Gary we expanded the rail system to carry the full scope of The Defender. He produced several prototypes, even making them in an array of colors including a pink version we named "The Girlfriend". We attended trade shows and conventions and found that lots of people were interested. That business was just beginning to take off when I was diagnosed with multiple sclerosis and had to cut back on my affiliation with Gary and Creative Sales. Much to my frustration, the needs of my health kind of put the kibosh on what seemed the promising reinvention of a post-retirement career.

The continued progression of MS has removed my ability to be physically active, something that's been a defining part of my nature all of my life. But I refuse to let it get me down. I'm most likely guilty of ignoring or pushing through early symptoms of the disease for several years before my diagnosis. I'm also likely guilty of believing that I was pretty invulnerable. As you've learned, I have certainly survived a number of incidents in my life that probably should have killed me. I'd say that on the whole I've been dealt more than my share of winning hands over the years, and I'd like to think I've played those cards well.

Of course, sometimes the dealer just gives you a bad hand. Life is a gamble, after all. That's true for all of us. The disease may have stolen my legs and restricted other movement, but I don't let it define me. I'm no victim. Ultimately, considering how debilitating the disease is, I had good fortune; its symptoms didn't become severe enough for diagnosis until I was in my mid-seventies. Until just a few years ago I had the gift of a strong and able body. I like to believe that gift was an accessory to a potent will and a capable mind. I was born to parents who believed in me and encouraged me to go after anything I ever wanted. I think often about my parents. My mother demonstrated the kind of strength and resiliency that I draw on when days become tough and I grow frustrated with having legs that no longer work. The lessons my dad taught me—about survival, woodcraft, independence, humor, toughness, focus—made my life and my career possible. Some of his lessons, direct and indirect, took me decades to learn fully. From my earliest days I was provided the tools—skills, knowledge, and instruments—that in turn opened doors for me wherever I went. An ability to shoot with speed and accuracy and the mental tenacity to pull the trigger when needed have earned opportunities for me that most could never imagine.

There's no arguing that it's been a good life and a wild ride. I've known the love of four amazing women. I've been graced with four loving, accomplished children and three step children. My life has been filled to overflowing with good friends and grandchildren. And I've had mentors and colleagues who never wavered in their support and belief in me. Because of the abundance of these people in my life, I've tried to make a difference wherever I could. I've tried to step up when asked. And I've tried to have a good time while doing it.

Over the course of my professional life I've worked hard to try to save lives, helping to design and implement measures that ensure the airline industry can protect its passengers from bad intentions of those intent on doing harm. By my best guess, I logged something on the order of 30,000 flight hours as a pilot, safely transporting tens of thousands of people to see loved ones, earn a living, take vacations, change their lives, start relationships, take new jobs, and see the world. I flew three decades without a mishap. Air travel had become an integral part of modern life and I thrived in its tumultuous industry. I'd like to think that some things the industry and the government implemented in the realm of security is based on my thinking and my advocacy—and that it saved lives.

Working in capacities beyond the cockpit, I've been shot at and I've done the shooting. I've taken lives, and in the process, I've saved others. I survived a war. I've built houses and shops and outbuildings. I've rebuilt and repaired engines. I've probably built over 300 guns nearly from scratch and repaired or refurbished nearly 2,000 more. I've designed weapons. I've written thousands of pages of position papers and procedures and protocols. I've offered the opinions I've formed on security measures in editorials and articles. I've testified before congressional committees. I have lived through circumstances that should have killed me. I have traveled. I have loved. I have lived.

What's the common denominator behind all the things I've done in my life? Nearly the whole of my life has been dedicated to following flight paths of one sort or another. The flight paths of airplanes. The flight paths of bullets. If you were to plot the trajectory of a bullet on a graph, one fired at the kind of distance only snipers must calculate, it wouldn't look a whole lot different than the glide path of an airplane.

When I talk about the flight paths of my life, of course I am speaking metaphorically. But don't discount the literal as well. Consider this: At their core, guns are objects that launch projectiles at high speed. The first guns were just tubes loaded with an explosive and a projectile. Similarly, even the most sophisticated airplanes are little more than metallic tubes mounted to a pair of wings with a few creature comforts and a whole lot of wiring and hydraulics thrown in for good measure. The purpose of both inventions—the gun and the plane—might be at odds but they apply a lot of the same principles.

What many people think of as a bullet is actually a cartridge that include the bullet, a casing, powder, and a primer. The primer is ignited, which causes a small explosion, which then burns the rest of the powder, creating pressure that moves the bullet down the barrel. A jet engine sucks air in at the front, combusts gases in a calculated series of controlled explosions that expand and blast the resulting pressure out through the nozzle at the back. As jets of gas shoot backward, the aircraft is thrust forward, not so unlike a bullet. My life has felt similar to that shared elemental action of bullets and airplanes for as long as I remember—a series of events that have thrust *me* forward.

Maybe I've had a few more unpredictable "explosions" along the way than most others. It has been a life fueled by—probably even guided by—both inventions, and I've tried to put them both to good use. I've followed those flight paths to their logical ends. I'd say I've hit the target and stuck the landing about as well anyone could expect.

Acknowledgements

I was always better at completing missions than writing reports about them, however, with careers in security, aviation, law enforcement, and the military, I've written a whole lot of reports. All that time at a typewriter and still none of it fully prepared me for writing a memoir. I certainly could not have written this book without a lot of help from others who, for reasons I don't entirely understand, believe in me and have stood by me. I'm not one to shy away from the spotlight but writing your life story kind of makes you feel like you're wearing drop drawers and you forgot to put your flap up. If you've made it this far, I guess you found something of interest here and I am grateful to you for reading.

I started writing what would become this book in 2016, mostly by trying to get my earliest memories on paper. It wasn't long after that I was diagnosed with MS, which complicated writing greatly. I regret that some of my memories could not be fuller and more detailed. MS can be a disease that tests you and too often it has robbed me of an ability to remember the past with the detail I would like.

This book certainly would never have been written at all if it weren't for my wife Jeannie. Not only was she the force under my wings that gave me lift, she provided the thrust to keep me moving. Jeannie saw value in my life and believed that my story should be told. Much of this book was written in the midst of the COVID-19 pandemic while I have been in a skilled nursing facility. Jeannie was my faithful companion during those trying times when we could be no closer than a phone call or a visit at a window, yet she kept the book moving forward, even literally reading chapters out loud and coordinating calls with old colleagues, my editor, and others.

A whole host of others, family, friends, and colleagues have helped me write this book by retelling stories they either lived through alongside me or heard enough times to have them stick in their memories (like a burr under their saddle, I suspect). I am forever indebted to their generous gifts of time, conversation, and storytelling, as well as their willingness to pull an old man along when his memory lets him down. I am blessed with the love and support of family. Among those who directly contributed to this book are my children Stephanie, Judd, Sarah, and Meagan, my second wife Beth Lindseth, my cousin Edith Ann (Edie) Connors, and of course, Jeannie.

I would not have been able to write this book without my editor, Mark Leichliter, who heard my stories, heard meaning in my life, and helped me find the words to allow others to hear my stories. The writing was made immensely better through under the sharp eye of Ann Marie Rozum. I am also appreciative of careful reading from my daughter Sarah and from Al Czarnowsky.

Among good friends, a champion of this book and someone who knows me about as well as anyone on the planet, I'm beyond grateful to my fellow Northwest pilot and airline security expert Peter Reiss. I never had a brother, but Peter is about as close to one as I'll ever get. Other great friends from Northwest and from ALPA who were of tremendous assistance in making this book a reality include David Williams, Jim Andresakes, and Jerry Wright. Among the many law enforcement and security experts who, once again, came to my call, were Denny Dillard, Howard "Butch" Luker, and Thomas Austin. There are countless more friends and colleagues who have contributed to the book in small but important ways and literally thousands of friends who have helped shape my life. Any omission of thanks to those who provided assistance in writing this book is a failure of memory, not one of gratitude.

About the Author

Captain Stephen A. Luckey is an internationally recognized airline security expert. Steve retired from a thirty-three-year commercial flying career as an International 747-400 captain with Northwest Airlines. He chaired the National Security Committee for the Air Line Pilots Association for eleven years, including the years immediately following the terrorist attacks of September 11, 2001, representing the security interests of 67,000 pilots. Captain Luckey's military aviation career included duty as an aircraft-carrier qualified US Marine attack pilot, flying numerous combat missions in Southeast Asia. While in Vietnam, having trained as a forward air controller and a special operations combatant, he was selected for duty as a psychological warfare specialist and counterinsurgency operative. In this capacity he served with the Korean Marines, Army of Vietnam, and other special operations units including the elite USAF Air Commandos. He saw extensive combat duty on the ground as a special operations commander and was the originator of the highly successful Kit Carson Scout Program, conceiving and implementing the concept of utilizing repatriated Viet Cong for specialized counterinsurgency warfare missions. In recognition of this work, he received the Bronze Star medal with Combat V. In addition to his military and airline experience, Captain Luckey was active in numerous anti-terrorism schools, trained with the FBI in aircraft-related SWAT procedures, and was a sworn deputy sheriff. He was also a licensed outfitter, a firearms instructor, and an acclaimed gunsmith. An award-winning graduate of the University of Pennsylvania, East Stroudsburg, he holds a BS degree in mathematics and physics.

Captain Luckey served as a member of the baseline working group of the Vice-Presidential Commission on Aviation Safety and Security and FAA's Scientific Advisory Subcommittee. He has addressed the US Congress Aviation Subcommittee on passenger interference issues, the US Senate Commerce, Science and Transportation Committee, the International Congress of Aviation Organizations, the US Attorney's Office, and numerous other federal law enforcement agencies. He was the US representative and former vice chairman of the International Federation of Air Line Pilots Security Committee. Captain Luckey played a significant role in the creation of the Federal Flight Deck Officer Program, which provided lethal force capability in commercial airline cockpits.

He has appeared on several popular television and radio shows including *Good Morning America, The Today Show, 60 Minutes, 20-20, Inside Edition,* and *America's Most Wanted.* His articles have been published in several books and periodicals and his commentaries have appeared in publications throughout the US and abroad. In honor of his long aviation security career, Captain Luckey was presented with the FAA Associate Administrator's Award for Civil Aviation Security and the Air Line Pilots Association David Behncke Lifetime Achievement Award, the highest honor ALPA can bestow on a member of the organization.